A Walking Tour of Lincoln Road, South Beach

Ask a Local

Kevin and Rebecca Plotner

Schiffer Publishing Ltd

4880 Lower Valley Road Atglen, Pennsylvania 19310

Other Schiffer Books on Related Subjects

Art Deco Architecture: Miami Beach Postcards. Paul Clemence
South Beach Architectural Photographs. Paul Clemence, with Foreword by Michael Hughes
South Beach Deco Step by Step. Iris Chase, Susan Russell, Photographer
South Beach: Faces and Facades. Iris Garnett Chase & Gabrriele Schuetz
South Beach Postcards. Susan Russell
South Beach: Two Decades of Deco District Paintings by Mark Rutkowski. Mark Rutkowski

Library of Congress Control Number: 2007929264

Designed by Bruce Waters
Type set in Futura Bd/Zurich BT

ISBN: 978-0-7643-2721-6
Printed in China

Published by Schiffer Publishing Ltd.
4880 Lower Valley Road
Atglen, PA 19310
Phone: (610) 593-1777; Fax: (610) 593-2002
E-mail: Info@schifferbooks.com

In Europe, Schiffer books are distributed by
Bushwood Books
6 Marksbury Ave.
Kew Gardens
Surrey TW9 4JF England
Phone: 44 (0) 20 8392-8585; Fax: 44 (0) 20 8392-9876
E-mail: info@bushwoodbooks.co.uk
Website: www.bushwoodbooks.co.uk
Free postage in the U.K., Europe; air mail at cost.

Dedication

To Gage and Cooper. You shine light on fun.

Acknowledgments

Heartfelt thanks goes out to all the people and researchers who have gone before us. Countless hours go into preparing a book but none can compare to the time accumulated in oral interviews and research that make up historical stories and documents. Without tracked history, today has little flavor. Meager letters and words cannot express the solid ground writers put together from haphazard happenings along the way. Mixed together and stirred, order is created out of chaos. Thank you to all these writers who have paved the path, tracking life with words, providing a historical trail.

Special thanks goes out to the Historical Museum of Southern Florida for all their patience and dutiful work. Regular every day people donate small clips of history to you for preservation and safekeeping, you are trusted with documenting life. Your work is rightfully noticed as you diligently change lives through tracking cut up newspapers and invaluable correspondences. You don't only track history; you offer it to the world.

Accolades and enthusiastic applauses to the Miami-Dade Park and Recreation Department. You have gone above and beyond any call of order. Aileen Landry, Chris, Vic, and all the hardworking underpaid over pleasing workers that make up our community, well done.

Our extended appreciation goes to Marlin and Jean as well as the loving and motivating family you have orchestrated. You've been encouraging and stimulating.

Bows of appreciation thankfully go to Baci and Dzia Dzia. From the cement that concretes our world to the five-minute work-enabling distractions that only a phone call or letter can provide. Everything between the two is too numerous to mention. Many thanks to you both.

To Tina Skinner and all her patient responses and encouraging words, golf clap to you. Gratefully to all the locals we've asked along the way...we tip our hats to you.

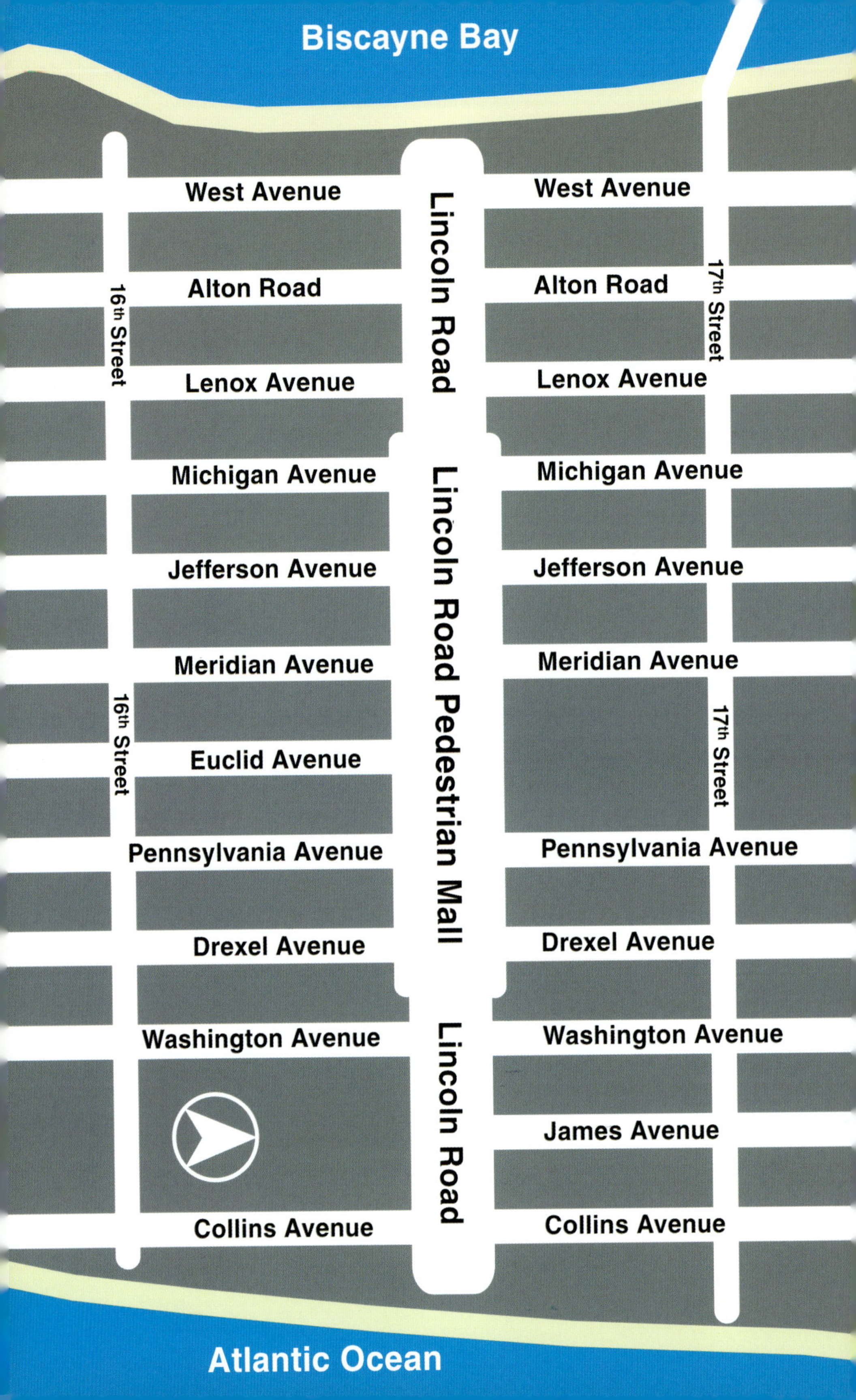
Biscayne Bay
West Avenue
Alton Road
Lenox Avenue
Michigan Avenue
Jefferson Avenue
Meridian Avenue
Euclid Avenue
Pennsylvania Avenue
Drexel Avenue
Washington Avenue
James Avenue
Collins Avenue
16th Street
17th Street
Lincoln Road
Lincoln Road Pedestrian Mall
Atlantic Ocean

Contents

Introduction

Ahhh... you're here.

The brilliance of South Beach is encompassed by the glamour of an international community, celebrities, models, and the potential of being somebody – somebody big. Wrap it all up with the glowing aquamarine goddess that stretches her liquid glory for miles upon miles and you have South Beach. Welcome to a high-class standard available nowhere else in America.

A quick visit or even perhaps a new home stands as unknown ground. A large number of us came for a visit but quickly decided to stay permanently. It's easy to become sold on the beauty and relaxed atmosphere of the beach that sits upon a worldwide trade port. The big city on the beach is a productive business world on vacation. Productivity is increased because the urge to get away for a break doesn't exist. Paradise provides.

The "island" is sliced by one of the most famous roads in America, Lincoln Road. This road is clearly the spine to the city. Originally is started out as a traditional road traveled by cars and jaywalked by pedestrians, but then in the '60s it was transformed into what we see today, a pedestrian mall.

The Lincoln Road Mall is laid out in a very easy to follow pattern extending from the Atlantic Ocean to Biscayne Bay. It's a true strait line from East to West. The road is broken up by cross streets heading North and South. Each cross street divides the mailing address numbers. If the address is 100 Lincoln Road or any number in the 100s, it's on the first block. If the address is 200 Lincoln Road or any number in the 200s, it's on the second block heading West and so on to the twelfth block containing numbers starting with the 1200s.

This popular stretch of shops, restaurants and businesses is more than a mall, it's the place to be. Lincoln Road has been coined "the people watching capital of the world." The place to be is also the place to be seen.

The best way to get to know a place is to ask a local. So here we go.

Chapter 1
The Atlantic Ocean

The warm surf of the Atlantic is often found relaxing sore muscles with a comfortable temperature in the mid-eighties. On average the air temperature hovers at 75, the water basks at 74. Perfection.

Paradise with a light breeze creates easy white caps.

The water color changes as the seafloor sand is churned in the mix.

In the summer months the water is often calm and flat as glass. In the winter the water runs on a cyclical rhythm for the most part. The waves gradually grow to aggressive surf over a matter of days, sometimes even reaching twelve feet high. This is often followed by calm waters that often flow flat. Overall, they grow higher, higher, higher, and then suddenly two days later it's flat. The calm waters usually stick around for a couple of days and then they gradually grow higher, higher, higher again. The variety is great.

Certain things are seen here that are never exposed to the rest of the country. South Florida is a different world from the remainder of America as well as the rest of Florida. The people that make up our great city are an ideal window to the world only topped by one thing, our vibrant waters.

The glowing aquamarine coastal shore is lovingly known and labeled as The Gold Coast. The reason is simple; the ship wrecks. As this part of the country was developing, many ships went down off shore. In fact our slice of ocean is littered with thousands of lost ships. Even the ones that have been found still have treasures missing. When a boat goes down, its contents are at the mercy of the water and the current. Valuables travel in many different patterns and directions depending on the activity in the area. Storms, especially hurricanes, stir up the waters and bring more potential valuables to the surface.

About a hundred yards west of where the sand and water meet, a sunken boat washed ashore and was found years later buried deep in the sands below the now Decoplage. This is a historical fact representing the times. Long ago settlers were wary and cautious of the ocean waters. It represented a power of the scary unknown and uncontrollable. It kept coming at them. Coming, coming, coming, higher, closer, advancing every day into an unknowing future. No one knew when it would stop. It was a mystery that it only went so far and then receded. It was a lot of water with deadly potential. The whole concept was frightening.

The decision to back off was deemed wise as people settled on the mainland. Soil was firm beneath their feet unlike here on the beach where miles upon miles of land was wet and soggy with bogs and swamps. At that time the island was a soft sandbar, not a solid block of land divided and quartered.

Any brush that floated in was welcomed as a breakwater barrier protecting homes, children, and families from the mysterious and

Four days later the water is like glass.

powerful ocean. Mangrove trees took root as their seeds floated aimlessly. Driftwood piled up against haphazard brush and sunken ships appeared out of nowhere and were left to rest. The more the merrier. Ships went down and they went down frequently in this early time of open seas unprotected by The Coast Guard and patrolled by planes. A lost ship was a common tale. A vessel floating in carried potential supplies. The population of Miami was slim for many years but the ships still sunk as the waters were traveled.

The nearby Biscayne House of Refuge in the 72nd Street vicinity, where the community band-shell now stands, was erected by our government specifically for shipwrecked seamen. This safe house welcomed wayward travelers in the late 1800s. The land was speckled with residents, Indians and alligators – little else. The House of Refuge was a welcome sight to a downed seaman. The Great Florida Reef, right off our shoreline, is considered a very famous graveyard of numerous ships.

To the south of the Lincoln Road beach access, is the inlet to the port known as Government Cut. Back when the century was young a large ship stopped up the port for days after it crashed into the shallows. All other boat traffic was halted until the mess could be recovered. Many of the early pioneers prospered with recovered goods from sunken ships. Building lumber was not readily assessable in the area making salvaged wood a valuable resource. Lumber was so scarce that many early settlers had only the framework of their homes built and then stretched canvas over the skeleton.

While a great number of ships sank from bad weather and countless other mishaps, some were sunk on purpose. As you look out into the water, an enormous artificial reef makes up a vast diving encounter. In the deep waters off shore, scuba enthusiasts can still make out the outline of tanks, submerged concrete, and sailing vessels. The objects have been covered over the years with limestone buildup, corals and wildlife. The Wreck Trek is a popular site for beginning divers wanting to explore the strung together formations. More advanced divers can go deeper or explore the old radio antenna that has been dismantled and welded into nineteen different pyramids. A sunken tugboat is added to the numerous fishing vessels that lay rest on the ocean's floor. The still, quiet, deep is teaming with colorful fish, disguised life and lurking danger.

One of the most valuable sunken ships ever found was searched for in our waters for nearly twenty long years when finally it was found closer to Key West. The artifacts of the *Nuestra Senora de Atocha*, or *Atocha* are on display in Key West. The Spanish galleon was transporting countless treasures of gold and silver, bronze cannons and more. Diving treasures are still found today from the bountiful *Atocha*. Another craft was found after The Hurricane of 1926 when residents emerged from their homes tattered and torn only to find a surfaced sunken ship a new addition to the local hotel's ocean facing sitting porch.

When you ask a local, is there gold out there today? At the end of 2005 I found something right at the foot of Lincoln Road while looking for smooth stones. A ring washed in on a wave literally dumping itself at my toes with twenty-one ocean-weary diamonds, grubby and dull from an unknown history.

In the water, the ground floor is always changing. If you're not happy with the distance or depth of the sand bar, just wait a few days; it'll change. You can feel it sometimes as you stand at the shoreline, the replacement and movement of sand at your ankles is clearly relevant. This movement carries valuable sunken treasures far from any submerged vessel and makes any location a valuable find.

The valuables have been bountiful and often loaded with importance but beware, not all treasures have equal weight.

Some wash-ups have taken form as ancient history but raise an eyebrow nonetheless. Years and years ago, the city sewage system dumped the end of the line pipe several miles out into the waters. It was the perfect recycling spot, according to them, mostly because it didn't affect their budget. The pipes dumped the raw sewage, along with everything else flushed, miles upon miles out into the sea so it wasn't encountered here on shore.... or was it?

A former Health Department worker Pepe Menendez remembered his assignment of the beach department. He was digging through some old paperwork acclimating himself with the position and found papers on The Condom Patrol. This section of very dedicated Health Department workers cleaned the beaches of undesirable wash-ups every morning. Now the possibilities, or missed possibilities, are collected into the main sewer system and caught by filters. The Condom Patrol didn't have such luck over thirty years ago; instead they swept the beaches every morning to remove any beached latex fish before the tourists emerged from their restful slumber.

Though not much of a treasure for the men collecting these lifeless and limp swimmers, it was bountiful for the fishermen out at the end of the pipe line. It wasn't just our waters that contained such a find; this was standard practice on coastlines everywhere. In other countries it's still normal business to dump the sewer lines directly into the ocean. Fishermen know this and flock these sights for their potential catch of the day. It was prime plush pickings in the imaginary fish bowl. Huge muscle bound Kingfish and Snapper are bountiful at these locations. Yummy! Makes me want to dig right into a plateful of fresh, grilled, juicy succulent Snapper.

Outside of the treasures we see in our waters, one of the most important things to be aware of is rip currents. By far, we lose more people to rip currents than any other danger on the beach. The flag system at the lifeguard stands depicts the strength of rip currents. Green is calm, yellow is moderate and red reflects dangerous rip currents. No flags shows no lifeguard. More importantly is the second, very concerning: the purple flag.

The purple flag means something's in the water, specifically, some sort of dangerous marine life is present. No, there are no more encounters with the lifeless latex fish; instead we usually see purple balloons.

The **Portuguese Man-Of-War,** named after a ship, not the country, is the most commonly found annoyance in this area – other than giddy teenage boys with cameras on their cell phones. The man o' war is easy to spot since they don't float in the water; they sit on the surface like a balloon. Concern comes in the form of the dangling tentacles and which way the current will be pulling those tentacles. Steer clear of that area if you see one floating on the surface.

The Portuguese man-of-war hunts by floating by and stinging his prey with venom from his tentacles. The prey is paralyzed while the tentacles retract inch by inch essentially walking the immobile food up to the bell where it can be devoured. Because the bell is transparent, this process is visible, slow and gruesome while captivating. The bell is harmless to the touch. Surfers readily pick up Portuguese man-of-war by their bells and toss them out of range. The gas filled balloon is pushed like a sail across the water's surface as he floats by posing little threat to aware swimmers. Don't forget the venomous stingers are active when the animal is washed ashore to wither in the sun. When you see the purple blue balloon soaking in the rays on the sand beware not to step on the tentacles. This animal is a nuisance that provokes fear and horror in the eyes of most children... or does it? If you take a washed up stick and poke the washed up balloon, it pops much like a firecracker.

If you accidentally get stung, get to the lifeguard stand as fast as possible. They are equipped with the latest technology designed to deactivate any unfired stingers: white vinegar. Sadly, fired stingers will not be deadened by the powerful elixir but any unfired stingers will be trapped in malfunction land, unable to perform. The lifeguards are here for this very reason.

Sea lice are often present in tandem but the sea lice is not visible to the naked eye. You'll never know you have sea lice until later in the day. They die quickly on skin because they need moisture to survive but where a wet inviting swimsuit rests, they remain alive, leaving a red itchy rash. Benadryl and an oatmeal bath are comforting.

Outside of pesky wildlife, our oceans are filled with fascinating shells. The sandy beaches south of us are protected but our region is fair game for any shell hunter. The Florida Keys National Marine Sanctuary and Protection Act prohibits guests from little more than looking at the oceans treasures to our south but here the ocean offers a buffet of raw materials. On South Beach you can find a shell and legally take it home with you – Government Cut is the dividing line. The best time to go collecting is right after a storm when the seabed is freshly churned.

Sharks are always a concern in the wild ocean. According to our lifeguards, an attack hasn't occurred here since the '20s. But just because there hasn't been a shark attack doesn't mean they aren't there. Our lifeguards, in tandem with the Coast Guard, do a fabulous job of paroling the waters by land and sea. If something is spotted, swimmers are notified immediately. Tarpon and barracuda is what we see most. They'll swim right past you not considering you twice for dinner. They are attracted to anything shiny and glittering like jewelry, which appears as a flashing fish scale.

In addition to fish, our seaweed can save your life and provide hours of fun. The leaves of **Sargassum Weed** are sustainable food if you're ever stranded at sea, however; the tiny balls are lethal. These leaves are sort of a sea salad if you like that sort of thing. They can also stand as disgusting transporters of floating filth so be careful if you're intending to slap on a bib.

Sargassum Weed can float with enormous size, sometimes miles long. In deeper waters, fishermen seek out the large floating islands of Sargassum weed looking for the fish feeding on the restaurant of plants while finding shade. Microorganisms and plankton travel with the weed and attract deep-water fish. As the weed floats closer to shore, the waves break up the enormous sections of Sargassum Weed into smaller pieces. These smaller chunks are unattractive to large fish but remain a paradise for coin-sized swimmers.

When you see Sargassum Weed in the spring it's an indicator that the waters are warming. Sea turtles often accompany the deep-water floating islands looking for food. The batches that float in here are often filled with small crabs and shrimp floating atop the natural raft and small fish swimming beneath. If you scoop your hands under the floating pile of weed, you can catch them without a net.

Another common harmless sighting is in the form of a seed. Although they resemble green beans, they're **mangrove seedlings**. The mangrove tree is the only tree that grows directly in salt water. It propagates itself by dropping these beans into the water. They eventually sprout roots and grow right then and there into a tree. Mangroves are commonly used in sandy saltwater areas not only because they grow so well but also because of their intricate root system that is thought to hold the coastal region together in times of aggressive surf.

When left to grow they accumulate in collective points and form an island. Mangroves, as a landmass, are impenetrable as their root system

Double rainbows prove perfection on Miami Beach.

crosses and weaves in and amongst itself. They resemble a man with a hundred legs stretching for solid ground on which to stand. Underneath these mangrove islands grow bountiful harvests of clams while atop the trees a Mecca of snakes and roosting birds enjoy a slice of their own private heaven with few, if any, predators. These green beans are not the only treasure we encounter.

Corals and sponges are also lifted from the coral reefs by the aggressive surf. Corals come in many shapes and forms and have often been used as a viable resource in this area. The corals are made up of animals, polyps that excrete the soon formed limestone. The Limestone builds up layer after layer as it grows. This limestone, in the past, has been harvested and used as building materials for early residents. As you travel the town you'll find staircases, walls, fences and even houses made of this very durable material. Limestone is often shaved and used as pavers or tiles. The polyp villages give a fossil affect in the tile face. As you later venture across Lincoln Road you'll see the limestone pavers used as entryways as well as building façade tiles. An easily recognized coral in the limestone face is the brain coral, as it looks just like a brain.

Sea turtles are charming seasonal visitors but also rid the waters of Portuguese man-of-war, their favorite delicacy. Turtle mating season occurs from April to November right on the beach. Miami Beach is a natural nesting habitat for five species of sea turtles: the Loggerhead, Green Leatherback, Kemp's Ridley and Hawksbill.

One of the major dangers for mating turtles is the same enemy the manatee faces, boat propellers and jet ski activity. Turtles are often found severely injured or diseased by wounds coming from propeller blades. During our summer months when the water is more docile and invitingly warmer for the turtles, the jet skiers and boaters come out in full force – just off shore. This is the same time and place the turtles, male and female, meet to... get busy. The female then comes up on shore to lay her eggs.

The turtle nest is something you may not recognize as an actual nest since it's under the surface of the sand. If you happen to spot some eggs in a haphazardly covered hole and you're not sure if they're turtle eggs, ask a lifeguard. The eggs are a near match to ping pong balls; tennis ball size for the leatherbacks. One time a tourist a few miles north of here spotted baby turtles making their journey to the ocean, gathered them up, and kept them in a dresser drawer of her hotel room. The proper authorities arrived and released the tourist of the perceived harrowing responsibility. The turtles were released back to the ocean, (Hiaasen 2001, 9.) their original location, where they could carry on with their potential lives.

The beach walk runs from 1st to 21st St. and welcomes bikes and rollerblades. The wooden boardwalk extends further from 21st to 47th St. and welcomes foot traffic only.

Baby turtles make the treacherous journey from the nest to the ocean shortly after they are born. Like birds, the struggle helps them to survive but still only a few will endure to mature adulthood. Most nests are buried a foot or so deep but some are only a few inches below the surface. Hot chicks, cool dudes is the local parks catch phrase explaining warm sand produces more females and cooler sand produces more males. Of the seven different varieties of sea turtles, all are currently on the endangered list. One historic fossil shows a turtle larger than a Mini Cooper while the largest live turtle found was over nine feet high and weighed over 2,000 pounds.

The Atlantic Ocean is not just wild territory for countless forms of life, it has long provided relief from the heat. One obvious form of controversy has plagued our beaches for years, topless bathing. Although clearly defined in our law books, the city understands the tourist community is the lifeblood to the area. The large numbers of international visitors are what make this community great. As the early settlers developed the land, the issue grumbled and grew until it was reported in the local papers. The final stand became one of tolerance and acceptance with action taken only from complaints. Now it's normal every day life and is known to the rest of America as a whispered phenomenon.

Today, there really are no rules at all. Straight, strapping men from over seas wear pink thongs high on the thigh with no inhibitions, along with their puffed out chests and hairy bellies. Sun worshipping goddesses lie topless in Brazilian Bikini bottoms focusing only on the soothing heat permeating deep into her muscles. It's Miami. However, if you ask a local real harm *is* done and should rightfully be set straight. American women that vacation need to pick a side and stand firm. The gal that arrives in her amply covering bikini, pale and pasty, is on her first day found lying in wait. On her second day is found with her straps hanging from her shoulders and on her third day with her top off but her hands strategically positioned. Then the fourth day is lived with hands frequently dropped and her bottoms hiked up into the deep cavern of floss-land all the while bashfully watching to see if other people are watching her. This, my friends, is a disgrace and an embarrassment

Medjool dates, one of the toughest palms, produce date fruit that needs to be picked and fermented for proper eating fruit. In dry climates the dates are better eating right from the tree.

to human kind. Make a decision and stick with it woman! When it's not for you, you pain us all.

As you stand on the majestic beach, with the captivating water in front of you and warm sand alive with sparkling quartz between your toes, you can experience legal voyeurism at its peak. Or you can venture into the depths of mystery and countless questions.

Standing at this spot of the beach, you are in fact part of **The Bermuda Triangle**. If you connect an imaginary line East 100 miles to Bermuda, then South to Puerto Rico, then back here to Miami you've got the geometric challenge that has created more questions than most other spots on Earth. Disappearances have ranged from small planes and even military squadrons, to a 520-foot boat. The only answer appears to be the triangle swallowed them.

Many ideas have been tossed around trying to find the answer for the phenomenon. One thought is that of horizon blur. Some days a captivating sight occurs when the color of the sky, beautiful and clear, is a near exact match to the color of the ocean, beautiful and clear. The horizon is not clearly defined forcing pilots to rely on instruments, not standard practice. Another thought is the Earth's magnetic field alters instrument readings. It makes sense that a plane can take a drink, but that doesn't answer how boats disappear.

It's a known fact that Florida is the lightening capital of the world. Plus, we experience exciting weather patterns filled with waterspouts. Some people think black holes happen in the vast oceans like they happen in space. Ideas have been tossed about concerning a microburst accompanied by lightening. To make matters worse, variables differ under the cover of night.

Specialists have studied bubbles of methane gas erupting from the sea floor. Bubbles are released as a normal function of the Earth's crust; they rise up to the ocean's surface and create a lower surface tension. If a boat is sitting right in that spot at that very time, the weight of the boat could overcome the lower density of the bubbly waters. A plunge could be unavoidable with no reality of recovery. The questions are numerous and entertaining but the government says the abnormal disappearances in relation to the high traffic patterns in the area are not out of the statistically normal range. It remains a point to ponder.

As you leave the beach heading back inland, take a moment at the dunes. In the 1970s the ocean crept to this point. The vast area of sand that you now see was part of a beach replenishment project that brought sand in from the ocean depths and extended our now beautifully spacious beach. Further south on Ocean Drive at Lummus Park, the ocean came up to the stone wall which at the time was used as a break-water. In some places the ocean was approaching so close that many ocean front properties had their property boundary lines in the ocean. The Decoplage here on the corner across from the Ritz was commented as looking like a bridge across the ocean under construction. Another local hotel's pool was 100 feet into the ocean at high tide.

A clear visual of this is shown in early movies filmed here, like the proclaimed "documentary" *Scarface* for example.

By the way, you can drive past the house where they filmed the famous gun battle at the end of *Scarface* with the infamous line, "Say hello to my little friend." If you drive over the Macarthur Causeway, the first island to your right is Star Island, where the house resides facing the bridge. The all white two-story house with a three-story middle has perfectly groomed grass with an American flag on a pole as the only interruption. The causeway is also where they filmed the popular movie *True Lies* with Jaime Lee Curtis and Arnold Schwarzenegger. The movies filmed here are too numerous to list, some of the most successful are *All About The Benjamins, Analyze This, Too Fast Too Furious, Miami Vice, The Adams Family,* and *Goldfinger.*

Several film crews have been hard at work at the foot of Lincoln Road, as well as frequent photo shoots for the local model residents. The closest to this exact spot was Paris Hilton creating publicity for her first album in 2006.

Before you wander past the boardwalk you'll notice one of the cheapest but best working inventions of the millennium. The string. The string? The string. As it stretches across the boardwalk, pools, and miscellaneous beach access points, the string is vital. To what you ask? The pesky birds. Both seagulls and pigeons infiltrate the walking zones and bomb otherwise beautifully adorned individuals. The string keeps these zones clear of sloppy rain. Thank you string for all your hard work, thank you from us all.

As you continue across the new boardwalk you'll see the current resident oceanside is the famous **Ritz Carlton** of South Beach. Little more needs to be said. The Ritz is The Ritz. Long before The Ritz, the first dwelling on this spot was the home of F.A. Sieberling, of Akron, Ohio, president of Goodyear Tire and Rubber Company.

Whenever a big name is in residence, guards are everywhere, binoculars poke from the roof and hide in multiple windows. Security ensures a relaxing stay, often with protection flanking their every turn and pivot. Most often there's more security then is visual to the eye, as the plain clothed protectors lurk in the shadows.

The Ritz likes to entertain and keep history alive with synchronized swimmers, or water-mermaids as they call them, parading through the lobby and to the pool just like they did in the deco days. Dressed in their tuxedo bathing suits, they salute the days of yesteryear. This treat of bathing dancers is free and open to the public Saturdays at 4 pm.

At the bar is a once in a lifetime experience: The Star Martini. This is a one of a kind martini made with a few high rolling names like 150-year-old Grand Marnier, Dom Perignon, and star fruit. The order, which serves four

The Ritz Carlton along with the Decoplage flanks the base of Lincoln Road.

to six people costs $400 and comes with a corresponding bottle of Dom. What the heck, it's South Beach! You only live once, right?

On the south side of the road is another prominent location in history. Currently, the **Decoplage building** is used as residences and rentals but the history is extensive. This location was long ago the residence of early pioneer and all around real estate mogul, Carl Fisher. His home, **The Shadows**, was the first house on the street. Fisher is the one man responsible for the ground covered in this book. His legacy lives on with his fingerprint on every inch of The Lincoln Road Mall. A high-class shopping experience and playground for the wealthy of the world was his dream. Today, Lincoln Road encompasses all financial brackets and stands as the place to be on most nights. The shopping is plentiful for most stores, giving them the equivalent sales volume only seen on Christmas in other locations. The turnover is high as the overhead is consuming.

When Carl Fisher lived here with his wife Jane the atmosphere was much different than what we experience today. It was quiet then, sparsely populated but loaded with mosquitoes, crocodiles and alligators. The sound of the wind passing through the palm fronds mingled with the resonance of seagulls as they played on the shore. The ocean breezes filled the house with the sweet smell of salty air coming in the window. The quiet of the unpopulated area was filled with the rhythmic cresting and falling waves outside the windows.

Fisher's palatial three-story home complete with an elevator to his private thinking quarters nearly covered the same width of land the Decoplage now inhabits. The land comfortably took up the whole block with plenty of room for the tennis court, pool, and gardens. There was even a private area for his pet elephant Rosie, a practical joke gift from Ed Ballard, his former Ringling Bother's Circus friend. The dining room was large with French doors that opened out onto the sand allowing for evening entertaining on the beach.

The home was filled with royal décor including Lenox china that displayed orange blossoms. The house was filled with extra large plush furniture and a pipe organ stood in the entryway with two curving princess staircases framing the piece. The fireplaces were made out of coral rock large enough to walk into and have a private conversation. In Fisher fashion, the fireplaces were always ablaze – always – even on the sweltering hot days, because that was a fireplace's purpose. When completed in 1914, the home cost just over fourteen times the price of the average house. The price is reflective of Carl Fisher's desire for the best. The elevator that led to his private thinking quarters on the top floor was the perfect example. Elevators hit the residential market in 1929, a full fifteen years after Carl's was installed.

The adventure was not pleasant for young Jane. She did not desire to be a pioneer, she had a taste for the social circuit and yearned to be adored as a high-class wealthy wife. She had plans for Carl's millions amassed by his business skills marketing the headlight. When Carl dragged her down to Florida from Indianapolis she dreamed of social gatherings and international travel. Their first Miami home was in the growing city on the mainland, directly on Biscayne Bay. She developed friends, began to establish roots and entertain. Her dream was finally unfolding right at the same time Carl decided he could no longer sit still in his white palatial mansion and stare out his picture window at the bay. Carl was a doer. He needed to do something. He needed to create. He wanted to make something of that pile of brush and sand out his window. He had ideas, he had a goal to build a playground for the wealthy, he had plans of his own. Ah… women and their silly ways just got in the way of business and smoking cigars!

Jane faithfully followed her husband to this new island loaded with mosquitoes and rats. She set up house here on the ocean, sour that the elite of Miami were so far from her reach. It was two and a half miles across the wooden bridge from the city that Carl helped John Collins complete. Even though the trip was an adventure as the bridge was deemed The Longest Wooden Bridge in the World, it took a full day to visit. Jane lived with the scarce population, she lived with no running water, and she lived with her driven husband and his crazy ideas charging forward like a child with his new Christmas bicycle. Her new job became one of entertaining the world on vacation while they were shopping for a second home. Carl and Jane left the area in the summer time, retreating back to Indiana for other business including Carl's Indianapolis Motor Speedway, the now famous Brickyard. Pioneers that stayed in Miami during the sweltering hot summers made peace with the muggy air propagating moldy closets and shoes that rotted between each wearing. The time before the roaring '20s was productive, yet muggy, in South Florida. Air conditioning was a cool welcome when it arrived several decades later filling the average home with relief in the '50s. Until then, the very wealthy afforded ice blocks set in front of fans, everyone else bucked up, kept an easy pace, and enjoyed the shade of palm trees.

Carl worked hard to fill his dream resort. He cleared the land, filled in the land, rid the land of alligators and crocs, and even offered two cents for any cat to rid the land of the pesky rats. Cats arrived by the bag. He promptly put up hotels one by one; the first was on Lincoln Road. His plan was to aggressively sell his lots to wealthy vacationers. Fisher was an honest fair man who studied facts and used them to sell an idea. He took every opportunity for free press he could muster so the advertising bill was held to favorable numbers. Buyers didn't flow in; instead they were skeptical. Carl assured new buyers that the ever-feared possibility of a tidal wave couldn't happen due to the powerful force of the Gulf Stream just off shore. "Florida's Gulf Stream flows through the Straits of Florida at the rate of 14 cubic miles an hour or 500 times the rate of the Mississippi River at flood capacity." (Donated clipping Historical Museum.) He honestly relayed costs of shipping food and drinking water to prospective buyers, including breakage in transport.

Carl was a hard driving businessman with boundless energy and a love for fast paced activity. His mind ran full speed charging from one great adventure to another. He lived on action. Ideas ran through his head like freight trains. He was a man of accomplishment out to change the way America vacationed. From his dealings and writings, he desired greatly to make Jane happy but had a difficult time fully expressing his feelings.

As always, he was too busy at work. He had an island to sell. Fisher was known for his crazy antics specifically aimed at free advertising to plug his current project. Back in Indiana he was consistently in the newspaper with multiple stunts. His wife first laid eyes on him when he stopped the whole town from functioning and turned every eye skyward. He flew over their heads in a hot air balloon sewn together by his friend, Fisher dangled below the balloon sitting in his car. He later showed up in town having seemingly driven that very car from the balloon ride. He dropped cars from high-rise buildings, and then had a man waiting in the shadows for the car to fall, stop bouncing, who would jump behind the wheel and speed off. He raced cars against horses, and he even raced his friends while running backwards.

The best way to describe Carl Fisher's sales tactics goes back to his days as a young boy where he worked the train cars selling newspapers and books to bored passengers. Fisher fashioned a waist apron to hold the individual reading material and money. If a customer declined a purchase from Carl's quick sales pitch, Carl would quickly flip his waist apron up and down in front of the customer. This revealed a rapid flash of a hidden picture, a sultry and revealing female accompanied with Carl's immediate follow up response, "Are you sure? It's a good read." Ironically, Fisher was the highest selling book salesman on the line. In Miami Beach to boost tourist flow he sent up a larger than life picture of the beautiful beach along with frolicking girls in bathing suits to Times Square in the dead of winter. The visitors came in flowing numbers. Business ideas came simply to Carl, it was pleasing Jane that was the mystery.

To get a visual of what life was like for them here in the Shadows visit the Vizcaya Museum and Gardens between Coconut Grove and Coral Gables. Subtract the newly added air conditioning and add alligators to the grounds and you've got the real flavor of the land for the time.

Nowadays, here on Lincoln Road, our largest obstacle from wild animals takes the form of "dog berries," meaning keep your head down and avoid the brown spots on the sidewalk. If you forget, the smell stuck to the bottom of your shoe will remind you to keep your eyes open for the rest of the day. Dog berries are probably the single most common compliant of any local. Some towns complain of gangs, we complain of dog berries.

Lincoln Road, was in a way, Carl Fisher's driveway. He made plans for a famous shopping thoroughfare coming from the Venetian Causeway connector bridge right from the beginning. The bridge leads the pathway right to the Fisher home site at the end of Lincoln Road. Lincoln Road was a dream in Carl's head right from the start. It was soon to be a pathway of glamorous shops and high-class wealthy society for his wife to fancy directly outside her front door.

But the unhappy couple didn't live here forever. They divorced and the Shadows was sold and turned into a ninety-nine-year-lease, popular at the time. The house encountered several tenants, the first of which was one that surely boiled Carl Fisher's blood. It was turned into a gambling casino and nightclub, one of the things he abhorred. Gangsters were quickly making the beach their home. Al Capone was one of many who set up shop in town. Headquartered in Chicago, his main business product was alcohol during the time of Prohibition. Ironically, when business was executed in Chicago and bodies were found cold, Capone was here at his Miami home on Palm Island. The popular mobster referred to Miami as the sunny Italy of the New World. With his concerns in alcohol, Chicago was dubbed the wettest town while Miami was dubbed the leakiest.

After this famous location was shut down as a casino it was made into the Lincoln Manor Restaurant, a Kosher establishment. It then progressed to the first Hebrew Academy of the area and then was used as a parking lot. After that, the area was transformed into an apartment building, one that was fully equipped with air conditioning- a big sign of the time. This Henry Hoehauser building was half sold to future residents before construction started. Apartments rented for $136.50, a slight bit less than today's $1,800 **Decoplage**.

As the construction workers were digging for the apartment building's foundation they struck gold... err... iron... iron and wood. An old ship was dug up with a **cannon** aboard. The preserved skeleton of the boat waited patiently for countless years as Carl and Jane Fisher lived their lives overhead. The four-foot-long cannon, abundant and common for the time frame, was hauled away for clean up with the intentions of proper display in future years. The presumed boat's name, *The Squid*, was exposed as the only markings on the cannon. (Blonston 1965.) It's current home is unknown.

This new state of the art modern apartment complex was christened by Jane, many husbands later and dressed in high society fashion finally achieving her dream, in a way. She was again known as Jane Fisher since after several marriages she reclaimed her name at the courthouse. Jane cut the six-tiered construction cake to celebrate the new apartment building.

As you walk further inland, you'll pass the artwork display windows housed at **Walgreens**. This is a collection of revolving displays connected to the ArtCenter. Three locations are present further west on Lincoln Road where artists rent studios and work, visible to the public.

Collins Avenue

Collins Avenue was named after John Collins one of the first pioneers of Miami Beach who originally invested $5,000 in the area with a small group of other men to grow coconuts. Some on the first parcels bought here on South Beach in 1882 were purchased for .35 cents an acre. By the time they were wrapping up their purchasing spree a few years later the cost had risen to triple that price. That still appears to be a small fee for property so valuable today, but at the time it was still filled with a lot of swampy wasteland and considered a sandbar as a whole. Plus, triple the price is triple the price no matter what the numbers are to start.

At the time, the ferry was the only way to cross over the bay since only a handful of people lived here on the beach. Mail delivery started on a bicycle in 1905, shorts were unheard of, women wore full-length dresses at all times and blacks, whites, and Jews were blatantly divided by social classes.

When John Stiles Collins invested his money in the coconut plantation, he and his devout Quaker family remained in New Jersey where he remained an investor only. Miami is supposedly the only place in the contiguous United States that will propagate a palm naturally with the **coconut** itself used as the actual seed for the new tree. Over 2,500 different species of **palms** exist around the world. A coconut can float miles upon miles across the ocean, wash ashore in Miami, take root and become a tree.

The coconut when used as a seed can be propagated in several different ways. Two vital ingredients are needed, moisture and heat. You can float a coconut in a bucket of water directly in the sunshine and sprouts will appear out of the eyes. The eyes of the coconut are the doorway for the sprout and root system to begin their journey. Once started, the roots emerge from the ground zone perimeter stretching out like tightly packed straws reaching for water. Another way to grow a tree is to place the coconut in the ground with the eyeholes half out of the soil. With enough water and sun, it'll grow.

A young coconut needs to be removed from the tree for the ripest eating. The green or yellow covering over the hard shell can be sliced open with one full hack from a machete. The younger the coconut, the more water there is inside. The older the coconut, the darker the outer protector becomes as well as, more fibrous until it resembles tiny ropes wrapped around the nut. At the early stage the coconut meat is more of a pudding-like texture. As the coconut matures, the water forms into the thicker coconut meat on the nut wall. As it over-matures the meat becomes more of a spongy foam as it grows closer to sprouting roots. The coconut, like a watermelon, is cold inside even when it's picked during a sweltering day.

Coconut water is used medicinally as a natural diuretic. It is also sterile and often used for medicinal purposes. A young coconut's liquid is sweet but becomes more of a watery flavor as it ages. The whole coconut palm is a viable resource. The coconut is obviously food and drink while the shell has often been used as utensils or pottery as well as charcoal. The trunk can be used as a safe building material because it is not only strong but also fire retardant. Palm fronds are used as rooftops or stripped and used for basket weaving, floor mats or ropes.

The coconut meat, or white copra, can be hard-pressed to extract a valuable and expensive oil. This oil makes up roughly 20% of vegetable oils but is also used in margarine, cosmetics, shampoos and soap. The high level of lauric acid in the coconut oil is what gives soap the ability to lather quickly.

John Collins and the farming team made a serious go at their plan. Although the coconut plantation idea was fruitful, the venture was not. The men attacked their idea with vigor but, in the end, it was not successful. The coconut sprouts proved to be a fabulous buffet for the jackrabbits and rats. Collins came down from New Jersey to inspect his failing investment and fell in love with potential. He was a farmer and farming was what he would do. He bought out one partner and joined forces with another. Together they began aggressively clearing more land and planted avocadoes, vegetables, bananas and mangoes. He found the best success with tomatoes and potatoes while his trees matured.

A few years later the salty breezes overwhelmed the plants damaging the crop. Collins put in a tree line of pines to absorb and clean the harsh salt air. In this area, pines are known to grow quickly, often several feet in a year. Some of these trees are still seen on Pine Tree Drive giving the road its name. Collins's partners fizzled leaving him sole interest in the property from 14th-67th Street.

The avocadoes, also known as alligator pears, inspired the practical jokester in Carl Fisher. When Fisher ran into Collins, he would ask how his crop of alligator apples was coming, just to rouse the old man a bit. The joke wasn't so funny to Fisher after he found out in 1919 that Collins's avocados were known all across America, shipped at $9.00 a dozen and were a famous dessert at Delmonico's. The famous restaurant in New York, sold the dessert for $1.50, twenty-five cents more than the cost of a whole chicken at the butcher.

Collins was seventy years old with a stiff persistence and a plowing attitude. He was a hard working man at only five-foot-three inches tall but carried an impressive aura. The reality was he lost two crops and was again looking at square one with over 1,600 acres of land, filled with sandy soil and salt air. Along with his family, he developed his land to be sold as parcels and continued his farming. He lived to the ripe age of ninety, an age seldom seen at the time.

Collins Avenue is today a thoroughfare of beach resorts, restaurants and shops running parallel to the ocean. It stretches far north covering all of Miami Beach from the bottom of the island where the numbers climb one by one from 1st Street to 198th Street.

Years ago there was a difference between what you see to the north of Lincoln Road and what you see to the south of Lincoln Road. Like most things, it was all focused around money. People of means were to the north in houses usually affixed with maid's quarters and land. Successful celebrities and well-known tycoons were not uncommon in this direction of town. Firestone, Vanderbilt, Will Rogers, Lindsey Hopkins of Coca Cola, and Milton Berle all owned a parcel of paradise. Lincoln Road, at the time, was the dividing line of wealth and poverty. Lincoln Road was the other side of the tracks.

This coconut palm has a resident. Do you see him?

How about now?

The Spite Wall

Before you exit Lincoln Road and enter the official Lincoln Road Mall there's a brief moment in time vital to the designer of the mission. **Morris Lapidus, architect of The Lincoln Road Pedestrian Mall** holds his mark on the gossip table for one humorous occasion where he was the lunchmeat between two very rough pieces of bread. As a young architect he designed stores, not by choice but instead by financial pull. His first few jobs designing buildings happened here on the beach involving various hotels. His most monumental job was designing one of his first buildings, **The Fontainebleau Hotel**.

The glamorous hotel was built in the mid-1950s as the dream child of the well known builder, Ben Novack. At the time the beach was settled and functioning as a steady tourist resort. Nearly three-quarters of the beachfront land was developed with hotels, nearly all of them of normal means. The Fontainebleau was the new building on the block designed as the best, specifically for the top clientele of guests. In 1964 the James Bond film *Goldfinger* was filmed on site.

Before the hotel made its debut the area was embracing a functioning slower pace. Many of the older, original buildings were still productive establishments but for the most part, a great number of them were tired and crumbling. Some were lifting their paint skirts and revealing their skeletons.

Many people looked forward to the energy the Fontainebleau was creating. As they built the hotel, the spark was igniting a dwindling fire of beach enthusiasm. The cost to stay was handsome at $33.00 a day. Many locals rented cabanas for the summer months when the children were on summer break. The goal was not high-class affordability; it was high-class glamour.

The Fontainebleau opened with a promise of shiny new excellence brimming with celebrities. Jimmy Durante, Jerry Lewis and even Bob Hope lounged poolside drinking tropical elixirs equipped with mini umbrellas all the while cracking jokes.

At the time, segregation was in full swing yet Sammy Davis Jr., Louis Armstrong, Aretha Franklin and Dianne Warwick were celebrated performers entertaining the guests. Once the show was over, they had to leave via the back door and head across the bridge to the Overtown area of Miami, then called Black Town. The real trick was still in the performers pockets.

They were awake and buzzing from their show, not ready for a long restful night of sleep so they made their own jam sessions in Overtown. The real joke was the elite clientele at the Fontainebleau were seeing a high-class show at an equally high-class price but the better show was to be had in Overtown when self-consciousness was absent, inhibitions were relaxed and toes were tapping.

Laughter and smiles didn't always fill the rooms and corridors of the Fontainebleau, especially behind closed doors in the office. On the contrary, during the designing and building of the hotel, the attitude was much different. Not only was there a difference, but the squabble set many a conversation a twirl for many moons thereafter. Ben Novack, the builder of the famous Fontainebleau, hired the up and coming Russian architect, Morris Lapidus to put the face and makeup on the hotel. Young on the hotel scene, Lapidus was an

The Fontainebleau is famous for the curve of the building, groundbreaking design for the 1950s.

economical find for Novack.

The desire for Ben Novack was simple, he wanted a hotel aura to attract the high-class attitude of the shoppers that frequented Lincoln Road. Lapidus was commonly known as the man who saw what people wanted, then designed the project to fill the need.

Sadly, Novack and Lapidus didn't have a smooth working relationship, they often bucked in design. The two men had many conversations appropriate for any theater screen. The curve of the building, a groundbreaking design of the time, was often the topic.

Lapidus designed new forms, new shapes, and new ideas. He became well known for his inconsistency with tradition and rules. His designs flowed with permanence while the monochromatic flow was broken up by shapes, holes, patterns and waves. He used columns that didn't perform a function but were solely used as decoration. They were thin and decorative with gold fluted feathers bursting from the top as the pole met the ceiling. Lapidus loved curves and angles. In the main area of the Fontainebleau, he designed a staircase that had one real purpose, a coat check. A traditionally thinking individual wouldn't consider a coat check in Miami were summer is the main cash crop but Lapidus wasn't traditional. He made the coat check specifically for a moment of glamour. When guests visited the Fontainebleau they were dressed in their best clothes, wearing their most glamorous shoes and glistening with their finest jewelry. More importantly they donned their best wraps and fur stoles, summer or not. A trip up the stairs provoked a trip down the stairs where each guest was in the spotlight looking down on all the peasants. All the while the other guests were looking up at the descending procession of class. The staircase was a subconscious moment to shine. It was like receiving an award for dressing up for the night. When Lapidus watched the responses of the guests he got a chuckle, amazed that people got such a thrill out of nothing. They loved it!

Morris Lapidus tore up tradition with his new style. The public couldn't get enough, they salivated like dogs with each new project he designed. After the Fontainebleau hit the scene, he was commissioned for project after project. His career was going strong at a solid pace of steady work.

The Spite Wall is famous for shadowing the Eden Roc's pool.

The Eden Roc and Fontainebleau have lived unhappily together since construction.

At a glance from the future, it looks successful but the powerful strife of the Fontainebleau is evidenced by a wall, **The Spite Wall**. After Morris Lapidus designed the Fontainebleau grounds he was commissioned to design the grounds of the hotel directly to the north, The Eden Roc. This sounds like normal every day business practices but in truth it's much more. Ben Novack, builder of The Fontainebleau, was the ex-partner to the builder of The Eden Roc. Needless to say, the relationship between the two men was not comfortable. The battle between these two became public when Lapidus took the handsome job of designing The Eden Roc. Ben Novack, in his fury, got in the last word by building his now famous wall.

The Spite Wall is well known in architcctural circles and even changed laws in some states. The wall is a solid sea of ugly concrete - pasty, creamy, dull, monochromatic, concrete - 17 stories tall, and broken up by hideous pipes extending the length to the ground. The over 300 Fontainebleau hotel rooms behind the wall have never seen the Eden Roc. This gargantuan beast of a wall covers nearly every inch of the hotel grounds from Collins Avenue to the Atlantic Ocean. All for the love of spite.

For the locals, the confusion lies here within, there was another wall. A 13,000 square-foot wall, the spa's backside, stood at the south end of the property. On this wall was a gorgeous mural of a stone pillar and an arched entryway. Behind the entryway were the hotel grounds, famous grotto pool and stone waterfall, hotel and ocean. The concrete wall, with mural, covered nearly the whole block and pictured the building and the ocean that you'd be looking at... if you weren't looking at the mural of the building and the ocean.

This was not The Spite Wall.

The Spite Wall was built intentionally to ruin the Eden Roc's pool which is the north wall of the Fontainebleau grounds, the mural was the South wall. The mural was a beautiful picture; The Spite Wall was solid concrete with only a few windows adorning the wall at the top, oceanside. This was Ben Novack's office. Surely he enjoyed many days at the office looking at his own handiwork: the shadow covering the pool. Spite, spite, spite, spite, spite. Ahhh.... it made for a relaxing day at work for Novack. In 2007 the wall is currently scheduled for reconstruction where it will soon butt up against a new Eden Roc tower.

Encounters at the Fontainebleau can be seldom topped. Eighty-one-year-old Molly Weeks said, "When I was younger, my girlfriend and I went to the Fontainebleau one day to the bar. We looked up and Frank Sinatra was sitting right there next to us. She piped up right away and said, 'Frrrrrrrrrrrraaaaaaaaaaann nnnnkieeeeeeeee, can I have your aaaaautoooooooograaaaaaaaaaph?' He didn't like that of course, but he was nice and still gave it to her. He had all these beautiful women hanging onto him, of course! He was Frank Sinatra! I went over to him later and asked him, Mr. Sinatra, can I have your autograph? He liked that when you called him Mister."

When locals went to the grand hotel for the day of adventure it was common to bump into a high rolling celebrity. That's what made the Fontainebleau so great. It wasn't rare to hit on a girl at the pool only to later find she was the wife of... or the girlfriend of... the place was brimming with icons.

Pepe Menendez said, "I approved the pool for the city. We had to give them variances because some of the stuff wasn't in the code. A lot we couldn't approve because it was against the health code. They wanted to do like in Mexico where the waiter would come serve you in the water but it wasn't approved."

The pool was well beyond normal pool size and standards. It housed a rock grotto with a second story water fall bellowing over and into the pool with enormous strength. The same waterfalls existed in the hot tubs. The pool was at least three times the size of a normal competitive swimming pool. One section had an island where you could take in the shade of the foliage and palm tree.

In true grandiose Fontainebleau style there was more. Years ago, another pool sat right on the ocean.

It too was a gargantuan puddle, at least double the size of a competitive 50 yard pool. But the claim to fame in this pool was different. Instead of the rock grotto theme, this pool was in the shape of a kitty cat. Although built as a kiddie pool, women were known to swim, sleeking around their men in cat-like form while they purred and quietly meowed.

After that, the **octopus** rose up on the scene.

This deep sea creature was made long before the foam-bumper shaped playground animals hit the market. The octopus was made the good old fashioned way- with concrete and paint. He hovered up above the kiddy pool at least a good seven feet in the air, floating as if he was performing a magic trick. The mere existence of the octopus invoked a festive atmosphere. His roughly twenty-foot girth was dwarfed by his enormous tentacles that waved out across the kiddy pool area. Underneath him was the flowing river intertwining in and out of grottos and foliage. As children and adults floated along, the octopus' tentacles sprayed down cooling water as you drifted underneath.

None of this equaled the water slide. The staircase was secretly hidden inside another faux rock formation stretching high above the octopus into the blue sky. The tropical plants growing in the rock face made the whole scene more realistic. After climbing the enormous stairwell, you stood high above the ground just below Heaven. You, and only you, stood right there next to God. You weren't standing on a balcony in a safe enclosed porch with a thirty-story building at your back. You stood in the open air. Air in front of you, air behind you, air to your right, and air to your left. It was almost like standing at the top of the ladder on the lookout tower with nothing to see but the soft smile of divinity shining down.

The view was not just the tunnel twisting down into nowhere, it was a vantage point. The rock at your feet bellowed the victorious climb of Mount Fontainebleau. In front of you were the tree tops creating separation from the vast aquamarine glowing goddess. The white curling breakers in the Atlantic matched perfectly the white puffy clouds overhead. The blue sky and the aquamarine ocean stretched forever and beyond. The smell of the green treetops twirled a dance with the tropical flowers. The perfume was green and light. The soft breeze and the ocean spray energized every inch of exposed skin. This was no water slide; this was the most beautiful view of the ocean known to mankind. This pedestal, 260 feet high in the air, offered a moment.

This moment was personal.

One deep breath nourished any exhausted body. One deep breath equaled thirty minutes of yoga, four aromatherapy candles, dozens of fragrant roses, and sixty minutes of deep tissue massage followed by a relaxing sauna.

That's where you could stand and experience calm tranquility.

This is the same spot in the sky where a few feet away was... the seething wall of concrete, sour with irritation and spite.

Chapter 2
Cross Over Collins Avenue

As you head further west on Lincoln Road, you'll notice this block remains a drivable street. **The Lincoln Road Pedestrian Mall** starts on the next block heading west at Washington Avenue.

Before Lincoln Road was transformed into a pedestrian mall, cars parked nose first at a 45° angle to the stores. At that time, the numbers of cars were much fewer than today. There were so **few cars,** in fact, that parking tickets didn't exist. Back before 1925 when the Miami Police Department encountered an illegally parked car they didn't ticket, instead they took the front seat of the car and held it captive at the police department until the car's owner bought the seat back in the form of paying their fine. (Donated clipping Hey, Let Go My Front Seat Historical Museum.)

Inside the **CVS Pharmacy**, you can shockingly find a great variety of international chocolate. They also do their best to provide a small amount of groceries. This is important to know since zoning laws restrict gas stations and grocery stores from Lincoln Road. (*The Miami News* 1958.)

This city block was long ago one of the most famous locations in Miami beach for one reason, the movie theaters. Although they don't exist here anymore, they made their mark. Five theaters lived on Lincoln.

Located at **230 Lincoln Road** was one of the most impressive and most famous theaters of all time, **The Carib Theatre**. Currently the location sits vacant and has been covered with painted plywood boards for years.

The former Carib Theatre, in its desperate state of needing attention, is asking rent of $1,792,000 for a year lease. The square footage totals 56,000, divisible once.

The Carib allowed a single screen showing for the customers sitting in its 2,200 seats. The front entry way was an elaborate garden lush with tropical flowers and green foliage. The floor and walls were covered with flagstone. The lobby roof was retractable while the garden included running streams of water and parrots that made the lobby their home.

Inside, the orchestra was well below the surrounding loge seats. The head of the theater displayed an enormous map complete with raised porcelain expressing mountain ranges, valleys and oceans. The auditorium walls, floor, and ceiling were covered in various murals giving an underwater feeling. The movie screen was raised up on a stage, extended all the way to the ceiling and nearly touched both sidewalls. The recessed screen sat under an enormous arch framed with heavy curtains and swags. The arch displayed a two dimensional octopus with tentacles reaching out to both sidewalls. When the lights dimmed for the movie, indirect lighting illuminated the octopus giving the appearance he was floating in the sea in which you comfortably sat.

Upstairs the mezzanine was enclosed in glass overlooking the lobby where guests peered down at those entering the theater. A television sat in the second floor lounge as well as another in the grand foyer. The 26,000 square foot theater was ultra modern for the time. A single drop of rain-activated sensors attached to the retractable roof and triggered the ceiling doors to close.

On opening day a band of military musicians paraded down Lincoln Road and filled the air with excitement. Searchlights filled the sky.

Multiple celebrities made appearances including Oleg Cassini and wife Gene Tierney.

The theatre opened right on the birth of the time air conditioning became readily available. It was first introduced to the general market through the entertainment sector for theaters and then progressed toward home availability. Newspaper advertising displayed an "air-conditioned" banner across the full ad.

During that time the theater was different than what we encounter today. Going to the movies wasn't what you did because the beach was too windy or a rainstorm was blowing through; going to the movies was an event. Actors made appearances at the premier and people dressed for the grand occasion. Women wore their best dresses and jewelry, wrapped themselves in furs and wore gloves. Many women appeared in sparkling ball gowns while men wore their best suits. Ushers in tuxedos escorted you to your seat after taking your ticket. It was an honored job to be an usher presenting glamour and dreams. He was well revered and certainly could support his family as an usher.

In 1954 "The Glenn Miller Story," made its debut here at The Carib Theater. James Stewart stared in the movie and appeared for the premier with his wife. This show produced a secret that wouldn't be unearthed for years. Construction workers uncovered a time capsule in 1997 when working on Lincoln Road repairs. The time capsule contained, "a screenplay from the film, a strand of pearls worn by June Allyson in the movie, and a menu from the Delano featuring a roast prime rib dinner for $3.00 and baked Alaska for two for $2.50." (Potts 1997.) The items were given to Wometco heir (then owners of the Carib) Micky Wolfson for his Wolfsonian Museum located at 1001 Washington Avenue.

The Carib Theatre closed down in 1977 from competition brought on by the big movie houses. The property sat vacant and sold in 1979 for $600,000, almost $72,000 below tax value. The new buyer, Mayer Haber of Miami Beach at the time, was vocal about the handsome profit he bestowed upon the seller since he was eager to obtain the property. He transformed the property into 26 retail shops each at $2,000 a month after a substantial amount of down money was paid. (Redford 1970.)

Chapter 3
Cross Over James Avenue

On the corner of James Avenue is a monumental hotel. The **Albion Hotel,** built in 1939 with Art Deco flair, is located at **1650 James Avenue**, with 115 rooms. Art Deco is a building style that flourished with the post World War I industrial age. During this time construction replicated industry. It was common to see things like metal steps, waves on roofs, and fountains frozen in concrete.

This architecture has birthed a private battle going on in South Beach unbeknownst to the majority of tourists. The two parties at war are preservationists and developers. The Miami Design Preservation League has done a stellar job with the preservation of Art Deco style buildings.

For some, it takes information to appreciate the Art Deco age. Often the design appears old and tired. Perfect condition or not, it resembles... Grandma, and everything in her house. It personifies slow, drained, aged goods stuck in the basement, filled with cobwebs and lurking spiders. In reality, Art Deco screams progress, action and trendy development. At the time the Art Deco movement was sweeping the country, the world was recovering from war. Death beyond numbers and financial ruin was changing back to traditional daily function sans war. The average person was living in desperation with little food and anorexic money. Thousands of people lost their jobs, unpaid electricity was turned off, kids wore shoes with holes in them, socks were darned and darned again. Clothes were recycled, food wasn't wasted and people certainly didn't celebrate over progress. Folks were busted. Art Deco defines the change in times to prosperity. Deco defines upturn.

The Albion Hotel is the most acclaimed Art Deco hotel on Lincoln Road.

Art Deco symbolizes the end of a painful time. Government battles were ceased. The burden families carried was slowly lifted. Theaters opened by the bucketful. Buildings were designed as a celebration. People began to work again and became more financially stable. The Machine Age represented progress and money. Daily life was filled with relief and recovery. This was all reflected in buildings styles. Each building had its own theme. One building was made to look like a rocket ship stretching up to the sky. Another building was made to look like an airplane or a cruise ship. Whatever the shape, whatever the form, they all represented new life filled with freedom and potential.

The Albion Hotel is the perfect example. The hotel symbolizes a large ocean liner. In the front lobby one whole wall is a **waterfall**. The hotel completely opens up and has an airy feel like you're on a ship's deck. The pool itself has portholes in its sides looking out into the arcade of shops. Some walls are curved like the head of a vessel while others are long and linear running down the length of a cruise ship. Chandeliers, deck chairs, tables, everything represents the nautical theme. This hotel shows the style and mannerisms of a regular hotel-not too fancy but just right.

Now they're famous for the perfect location smack dab in the middle of the Lincoln Road Mall, the Convention Center and steps from the ocean. The hotel is reasonably priced and clean. Complementary iced tea and water makes a lounging pool day more restful. If you ask a local, you're better off parking your car at the parking garage a couple of blocks West for $8.00 a day. The valet has to run a distance and takes a long time.

Right here, was another famous spot in the history of Miami Beach. When Carl Fisher was laying out the land for development he wanted to cater to high-class society on vacation. He built **tennis courts** here in an enclosed building with a glass roof. The building itself had ornate concrete and brick walls that supported the dome roof resembling an airplane hangar merged with a greenhouse. Tennis was the new craze. The average tourist didn't desire a luscious tan like today so a housed court was desired.

Fisher entertained celebrity tennis players and held many tournaments in the building. He had the players stay diagonally up the street at The Lincoln Hotel, at no cost to them. Big names, big competition, big newspaper articles to describe the grand affairs all equaled free advertising. It made good ol' business sense to Fisher. This was good publicity. Plus, it was a selling point for vacationing clientele to rub elbows with well-known tennis players of the time.

Elaborate **Christmas parties** were held here with a Christmas tree as tall as the building decorated with ornaments, tinsel and sparkling lights. Local children dragged their parents by the arm to see Santa. Everyone was dressed in their holiday best while presents arrived car after car. Highly adorned adults mingled, drank eggnog, and ate Christmas cookies. There was no snow outside and no one bundled up in mittens. Instead there was sand and palm trees, just like the original Christmas. (Fisher 1947.)

After a short number of years attendance at the courts dwindled. Carl Fisher decided to change the courts into a more useful theater. To conquer this transformation he wrote all land owners in the vicinity for approval since it was not permitted on their deeds. The response was favorable and met with enthusiasm. Fisher then sought an independent business to fill the theater, adding their own touches to increase the properties value.

The former Flamingo Theatre is currently used as an elite night spot.

Back across the street, the **Flamingo Theatre** was located on Lincoln a few doors west of the Carib Theatre. It was relatively small compared to the other theaters on Lincoln Road. The one screen Flamingo premiered first run movies, foreign films, *Diabolique* and *Gigi* were among them. The Flamingo met tension with the X rated movie *I Am Curious*. *The Miami Herald* refused to run the advertisement. After a few weeks, the paper succumbed to a one inch by one column print of simply the title and X rating. (Cinema Treasures)

The Beach Theatre was the third working theater on this block of Lincoln Road. Compared to the Carib Theatre and the Flamingo Theatre, it was more middle ground. It was nowhere near as high-class as the Carib but didn't fall too far behind. People dressed nicely in suits and dresses and wore hats presenting decorative feathers. But overall it was still more casual. The enormous lobby stretched nearly four stories tall. One full wall was covered with mirrors; another was filled with fake tropical plants displayed behind glass- all four stories. Admission was eighty cents. (Cinema Treasures)

All in all, the **theater is Deco,** alive with the bright neon lights and linear signs, wavy lines and geometric decals. The octagonal ticket booth, rectangular displays of movie posters and circular porthole windows all sang Art Deco.

Times changed and businesses either evolved or died. Air-conditioning became more prevalent in homes and was no longer a feature for only the movies. Large movie mega screens moved into town with multiple showings. The single screen theater became outdated. To keep up with expenses theaters looked for options, Beach Theatre morphed into a Yiddish live stage production house. The Jewish population on Miami Beach had grown strong reflecting accomplishment for the area, a positive sign from earlier days when Jewish people were shunned in Miami Beach when it was normal to see signs that read *Gentiles Only* or *No smoking, No dogs, No Jews*.

Chapter 4 Cross Over Washington Avenue

As you cross over Washington Avenue heading west towards Biscayne Bay, you are officially entering **The Lincoln Road Mall**. Named after Carl Fisher's favorite president, The Mall extends west from this point for a span of nine blocks to Alton Road. Lincoln Road Mall is an open-air pedestrian mall filled with numerous stores and restaurants from all over the world. This is one of the last surviving shopping venues on American soil that houses a cornucopia of retail outlets instead of being dominated by superstore storefronts.

This is one of the main reasons Lincoln Road is adored by most locals. The presence of mac-daddy superstores does not hound you on the mall. A handful of storefronts are nationally known chains but Lincoln Road still finds comfort with the mom and pop store. This valuable asset mixed in with the international stores working on the same concept gives the mall magnetism and distinction.

In 1960 this stretch of Lincoln Road, endured a $600,000.00 transformation when it became the first pedestrian mall in America. Prior to this transformation the road was 100 feet wide, 50 feet was dedicated to the road while 25 feet of sidewalk flanked both sides. Originally organizers desired music piped throughout the street. The transformation of the mall was not always successful. Some shop owners were thrilled with the idea and some abhorred the change. They fought a battle from day one.

As the street was under construction, a number of store owners prepared for the windfall. Many shop owners predicted the inflow of international visitors and prepared their stores by traveling abroad, stocking their stores with the best merchandise the world had to offer. Right from the start The Lincoln Road Mall prided itself with merchandise unseen in other stores across the country.

The transformation of the road from a normal street filled with cars, taxi cabs and busses into a paved sidewalk with decorative foliage was driven by one force, The Lincoln Road Foundation. At the time attendance to the shopping district was slim and needed a boost. Their goal was to put the people back on the street. The Foundation saw the statistical numbers showed over thirty percent of residents lived close to the mall; they just needed a reason to visit. In tandem with the Convention Center's proximity and tourists a transformation made business sense. New life for a new road seemed like responsible action.

Like most things, the idea was challenged by doomsday negative thinkers. Not all merchants on the road were willing to take the risky step. This created a long battle that endured several long years of discussions. At the time when the transformation was going up for the vote, the anticipation was high but the election outcome predictions were higher. Forecasted numbers ended up being far from reality. "Close to 80 per cent approval of Lincoln Road property owners is claimed by the Lincoln Road Mall Association." (Smiley donated clipping Historical Museum.)

The struggle originated in the usual form, money. The push to alter the road became so desirable to some shop owners they offered to collectively pay the bill if the vote was passed. "Their entire cost will be assessed to 59 property owners of 65 parcels of land along Lincoln Road. Other taxpayers won't pay a cent." (Finkelstein donated clipping Historical Museum.) Still, the discussion and vote wasn't an easy sell but drastic action was necessary to revive the street.

The issue was voted on and approved with a slim margin of victory. The predicted eighty percent approval was minimized with a fifty-five percent vote. A majority was reached and the project approved. The project was to be paid for by fifty-nine property owners providing the 232 retail stores on the street with a mall. The city parks department would be in charge of filling in the tropical foliage.

The well known architect from Russia, Morris Lapidus was hired to design the project. He had been actively working the Miami Beach area for a number of years prior to the Lincoln Road project and had built up a following by the time the plans were presented. It had been just over five years since his design of The Fontainebleau and The Eden Roc. He was responsible for designing a great portion of the buildings along the Miami Beach shoreline as well as some in Aruba and Jamaica when The Lincoln Road Mall project was on his desk. Lapidus is loved by many residents in Miami Beach partly because of his artful designs and partly for his accidental involvement in the Spite Wall. Nonetheless, his name has not always been associated with love and admiration.

The intention and blueprint of the Lincoln Road promenade was to be consistent with the **Miami Modern** style of Morris Lapidus known as **MiMo**. His design for the mall revolved around international flare supported by local ingredients. He chose Florida marble and native coral rock with a black and white striped concrete floor. The design was made to break ground in the shopping industry, display new venues and increase sales.

Morris Lapidus didn't think small. He wanted people to come to the area but he commanded them to come to his mall. "Lincoln Road must have not only the beauty of pools, fountains, shelters, gardens and tropical foliage, but features which will make people feel that no trip to South Florida would be complete without a visit to Lincoln Road." (Lapidus1958.) He didn't limit his ideas to just shopping and creating a mall area, he wanted the whole spectrum. Lapidus desired anything innovative or revolutionary to be shown on the mall.

He built museum showcase exhibits where displays revolved with newly introduced product. These show windows were used in the thoroughfare to move people along weaving them from store to store. Lapidus designed his plan around the potential millions of shoppers he predicted to flock to The Mall.

Raise the street and make a sidewalk sounds easy but the goal was not to build a larger sidewalk, it was to incorporate flavor and design with shopping. It wasn't just filling in the road cavity. The area needed electricity, watering systems and fountains including filter systems, pipings and underlays. Construction began August 1, 1960, with a completion date in November just before Thanksgiving. The job was well orchestrated. The Thanksgiving debut was no mistake or accident.

A groundbreaking ceremony was organized fifteen days after the construction began complete with bathing beauties and an elephant. This timing showed an embracing image of construction in progress.

When Carl Fisher first came to Miami Beach to develop the area he was famous for his pet **elephant, Rosie** a gift from his friend Ed Ballard, in Indiana who formerly owned the Ringling Brothers Circus. The elephant in the ceremony was a symbol of Carl Fisher and his antics. When Fisher first received the letter from his Indiana friend telling him of the coming gift he responded with a whoop! He was jubilant with the possibilities. Fisher was always looking for free advertising through newspaper articles and the elephant would be perfect. Even before the elephant arrived, Fisher hired a trainer and ordered jeweled headdresses for Rosie to adorn. She was indeed a success. He often used Rosie to haul concrete blocks for the camera or pull tree trunks from the Earth. It was all free publicity and he pushed the opportunity as far as it could travel. Later, after the area was a tourist Mecca he used the elephant for visiting children wanting an elephant ride. Rosie was such a successful asset; Fisher acquired another elephant and named her Baby Carl. The two animals worked together advertising the beach paradise.

Another elephant was used at the groundbreaking ceremony as a symbol of Fisher's pet. She wasn't just an elephant; she was a symbol of the whole island's transformation. She represented swampland, mangrove trees filled with wildlife, and mosquitoes. The elephant was coupled with a more traditional form of advertising for 1960. Miss Lincoln Road, Miss Lincoln Road Hospitality, and Miss Lincoln Road Progress wore sashes and swimsuits representing the sun and fun of the beach. Lincoln Road was undergoing surgery and any publicity could only shed light on the new beginning.

The groundbreaking was designed as an affair to bring press but also to bring customers. Their hopes were not grandiose; they just wanted to spread the word. They did everything they could to accommodate would be patrons, including free parking for the event. When the city gives the meter maidens a long lunch break it's a true sign of full participation for the goal of success.

The transformation of the street into a pedestrian mall happened with textbook accuracy. Electricians worked alongside gardeners while construction workers buzzed with accomplishment. The team embraced one goal and that was to get the job done.

As construction continued, businesses remained open. From the beginning, not all storefronts were in favor of the transformation. Some business owners became more nervous and irritated with their loss of business during the time of construction. This fueled their fury. For some, tension levels were high while anxiety levels boiled. All in all the transformation, including the votes to pass the adventure in elections was a delicate matter. Many stores held huge sales while construction progressed outside their windows. The dust was present and the noise was loud but businesses were there to make a profit. Construction of the pedestrian mall transformation made a dent on the already slim numbers in attendance. Fingers were crossed and prayers where whispered as shop owners waited for the hopeful flurry of business on November 26, 1960.

The carefully planned grand opening celebration was appropriately positioned right on the crest of the biggest shopping day of the year. The Thanksgiving shopping frenzy of 1960 was soon to go down in history. Event coordinators were hoping for huge attendance, confident a million shoppers would come to see the new mall. The grand opening ceremonies included a fine itinerary. Other towns across America were fixing their schedules for grand Christmas tree lightings; Lincoln Road Mall was scheduling mall lighting. A band concert and a fashion show were presented to attending guests. Area officials invited all the big name entertainers, sports figures, and celebrities they could find. Drinks and prizes were offered and musicians leisurely walked the street adding thrown festivity in the air like it was electricity.

The car-free zone was well received and attracted many new faces. The season was successful. However, when merchants were polled on the decision, not all voices were positive. Some commented on the lack of public restrooms, while others were just sour on the whole ordeal. "Old retired folks will clutter up the center mall areas, sit around, eat their lunches, read newspapers, cheapen the area. I'm hoping not – yet fearing." Other store voices were more factual, "Why, just the other day, I saw a woman take her little boy to a corner of the mall... and in full view of everybody, yet. Can you picture the impression tourists would get? ... I'm keeping my fingers crossed." ("Merchants Happy? Well, Yes... and No" donated clipping Historical Museum.)

Walking The Mall

Back when the road was first becoming engrossed with people, the daily procedures were run a little bit differently than what we see today. Signs were posted along the road reading "POLICE ORDER: no bikes, no skating, no dogs on mall." Thankfully, times have changed. At that time, fire and police emergency phones were sporadically placed around on telephone poles. All in all, the whole atmosphere was slower and more sedated – and of course, less populated.

Carlos Zapata's information kiosk leads shoppers down The Lincoln Road Pedestrian Mall.

At the official eastern entrance to The Lincoln Road Mall you'll notice a leaning **glass house** flanked by low lying pools and backed up by a pool, waterfall combination. Sadly, the half-glass-wall waterfall has been intermittent in function in the recent years. Although the concept is reminiscent of a glass house blown to a tilt by a hurricane, it's designed to look just as it stands. Some people incorrectly think this is also a work of Morris Lapidus when he designed The Mall. It's not. This art form was originally designed for a purpose by the famous architect, Carlos Zapata. Zapata also designed the new Publix Grocery store on the bay at Sunset Harbor – 20th Street and West Avenue.

According to Tourism and Cultural Development, Miami Beach Arts & Entertainment Liaison, Dennis Leyva, the glass enclosure was designed to be an information kiosk. The intention of the kiosk was for touch screens to provide information as well as offer the ability to purchase tickets on site. Today, instead of information, it stands as a solid – yet leaning – piece of art.

The first building on the south side of the street was the home of the Woolworth's store. The front of the store was covered in a natural **keystone** façade. This is the sister product to oolitic limestone found naturally often a few feet below the ocean's surface. **Oolitic limestone** is costly to harvest and over the length of many years, is difficult to maintain. The deep cavities in the product's surface have a tendency to take on dirt and hold tight. This is the reason it spontaneously supports plant growth.

The keystone that was used on the face of the Woolworth's, was discovered as a cheaper, less porous alternative used widely with Art Deco buildings in the area.

Woolworth's was popular. Even when criminals and low attendance hit the area the hardest, Woolworth's remained a strong retail store. This store particularly was doing fabulous business. "It had been in the top five Woolworth's stores in square-foot profits for nine years straight. It stocked three and a half times more items than a regular Woolworth's." (Stofik 2005, 134.)

F.W. Woolworth Company made one of the best nickel, dime stores known to mankind. They were one of the first stores to break the barrier of carrying every product line from bread to buttons and back again to makeup and gerbils. As business goes, Woolworth's morphed with the times and later changed to Foot Locker. So, in essence, the great store that America has loved through the years is still with us.

No, you wouldn't buy a wedding gift there, but where else would you go when you needed "window glamour with plastic draperies – durable and stain proof, just wash with soap and water, 90 inch long and 36 inch wide, including the valance, all for $1.00?" (Miami Daily News 1962.) Nowhere. Nowhere else, I tell you. Woolworth's was the spot.

After Woolworth's, **400 Lincoln Road** was inhabited by a high-class European style men's clothing store known as **Mark 400**. The glass windows that encompass the curve of the building on the corner were where the glass elevator took you to the second floor. You could stand in the elevator flush up against the windowpane and watch the traffic pass by as you rose up to shop. Talk about see and be seen, this was the staircase-to-nowhere of Lincoln Road just like Lapidus built in the Fontainebleau. Everyone watched you go up and down and you watched everyone else as you took the trip on display.

The true beauty of this spot was years ago, long before the Woolworth's and long before any of these buildings were on Lincoln Road. Back when the road was a single street, cut wide and paved with white coral, the gleaming white roadway was captivating and clean.

Sitting spots are not inviting per request by merchants to designer Morris Lapidus.

Carl Fisher built the **Lincoln Hotel** here on this spot in 1916. The hotel was one of the first structures on Lincoln Road. Even as late as 1920 there were only three major hotels on the whole island, one being the Lincoln Hotel. It was first built a little further up the road a few hundred yards; an addition was added to meet the tourist demand. The addition was larger than the original structure adding thirty-five comfortable rooms causing the grand hotel to cover the entire block between Washington and Drexel. The two buildings together took up the whole south side of the street. This hotel and Carl Fisher's house on the ocean were the main locations on the street at the time.

While the road was first being excavated by Carl Fisher and his crew of workmen, it was engulfed with unkempt trees. These trees were mostly overgrown mangroves impenetrable from the extensive root systems. They were all ripped out and the area was filled with sand dredged from the ocean, specifically the bay. Fisher's intent was not just to make land, he was concerned in making land high enough so that the building structures were above any storm surge that could potentially take the island. He focused on a minimal lift of three feet. The ground was then leveled and left to cure as it cooked in the sun. From there, grass and trees were brought in and planted. The resulting land was flat and full of sand, lustrous and white.

When the Lincoln Hotel was erected, there was beauty across the street. In the naked sand, they planted grass by hand with countless workers from Bermuda. The grass across the street was a beautiful expansive **golf course** stretching out for acres upon acres. At that time a guest could golf for $2.00 a day- not per round. Today the par three is free to beach residents.

To prepare the land for the golf course, Carl Fisher had dirt from the Everglades brought in load after seemingly endless load. With the extra fill he created hills and craters with the goal of making the course a challenge as well as aesthetically pleasing.

Shortly after completion, The LaGorce $10,000 Championship brought in well known golf pro's of the day. Spectators flocked to the area to watch the largest golf purse in the country. John LaGorce was not just the famous editor of the *National Geographic Magazine*; he was a good friend of Carl Fisher's.

Along the side of the golf course was a **bridle path** providing miles of pleasurable horseback riding. This rounded out Carl Fisher's whole plan and concept that he was making a winter playground where he would teach all of America to vacation. The high number of wealthy people making Miami Beach their second home grew abundantly. As they arrived, so did their horses. Fisher set up several stables around town to accommodate the horses.

The clubhouse for the golf course is now a portion of the current Community Center on 21st Street. Eventually the golf sensation died down to an uneventful attendance record. The amount of land used by the golf course was expansive. Carl Fisher saw the area could be downsized to one full size course and another smaller course instead of the gargantuan three courses. As Lincoln Road grew, Fisher wanted the whole road developed for high-class shopping. He made contact with his most aggressive lawyer, an ex-football halfback who played for Vanderbilt, Frank Katzentine, and laid out a plan. Katzentine later went on to become the Miami Beach Mayor who aggressively battled Al Capone. He is also the founder of the WKAT radio station, famous for filling the airways with big-band music and variety shows.

With the desire to change over the golf course, Fisher knew Katzentine was the man to get the job done. Katzentine quietly contacted a gentleman desiring to build on Lincoln Road and together they set up the plans for the building securing the construction materials and workmen without a peep. They were well organized with their project for a reason. They arrived on site all at once and promptly went to work putting up the building. They worked together like a well functioning team making no mistakes to waste time. Construction charged forth at a heavy pace without pause but instead with focused intention. "The civic-minded, golf playing people who opposed the building could have secured an injunction to stop the work, but they would have had to put up a bond which would be forfeit to the builders in case they lost the final suit. The more complete the building, the more money would be required as bond, and frequently, by the time the opposition could get up enough scratch to post a bond, the work crews would have made that sum obsolete." (Herndon 1954.)

The building was swiftly erected and opened as the famous Exotic Gardens where the newest addition to Lincoln Road sold flowers. The location, **607 Lincoln Road** is currently home to **Carnevale**. The construction of this building spurred the construction of three car showrooms, several retail stores, and clothing stores. They collectively attracted an impressive clientele. Saks Fifth Avenue, Milgrims, Delman's, Elizabeth Arden and even Bonwitt Teller made their homes on Lincoln Road. Together they clothed the wealthy multimillionaires of Miami Beach. One shopping trip could make their season, depending on the customer.

The remainder of the golf course was later sold to the city of Miami Beach, hence the ground for the **Jackie Gleason Theater of Performing Arts**, parking zones and **Convention Center**. Back in the '50s Lincoln Road was a popular place to shop; the parking spots at five cents an hour were favored.

Morris Lapidus was also commissioned to design the auditorium now named The Jackie Gleason Theatre of Performing Arts in his honor. Gleason used the theater a couple times a week, leaving other nights open for other attractions. One main show was fight night where well-known Cassius Clay, AKA Muhammad Ali, fought his way to fame. As Gleason taped his television show at the theater, he fell in love with the beach. Gleason's television show was another free form of advertising attracting tourists to the area.

The Convention Center was home to the Miss Universe competition running from 1960-1971. The contestants stayed at the Shelborne Hotel where they set their handprints in the sidewalk entrance. This competition is not to be confused with the less famous weekly competitions held with the vacationing beauties as the contestants. Miss Casablanca competed representing her hotel instead of her hometown.

In front of the Jackie Gleason Theater is the **Miami Beach Walk of Stars**. This section of footprints frozen in time is meant to honor celebrities and artists that have made their mark on our beautiful city. Recipients like Kelsy Grammer, Ann Margaret, KC and the Sunshine Band, Gladys Knight, and Muhammad Ali are all stepping on our city every day.

The tradition was initially intended to be displayed on Lincoln Road when it was started by Mayor Chuck Hall. His footprints were the first to be placed in a concrete block when he made a big production of the ordeal in a ceremony on Lincoln Road in this area.

Mayor Hall was known for a comment creating a quick chuckle. This relaxed people and often invoked a response in turn from locals. As he stood in the wet concrete one bystander said, "Hold it that way for a while, Chuck, we're going out to sea for the rest of the ceremony." (Eiland donated clipping.)

After the mayor completed his production of the foot prints and signed his name to the wet concrete he continued his moment in the spotlight with a production of cleaning the wet concrete from his feet. As the crowd watched his mini-show Mayor Hall said, "Folks, you must come around sometime when I'm taking a shower." (Eiland donated clipping.)

Although the footsteps were originally planned for The Mall, they were relocated at the Gleason Center where they are now seldom seen in comparison.

The golf courses served many purposes over the years but is probably most famous for one publicity photo showing an elephant as a caddie. When Miami Beach was in the financial throws of trying to survive the struggling economy, Carl Fisher pulled yet another publicity stunt. President Elect Harding was coming to the big city of Miami as part of his campaign rounds. Fisher, through his unending connections, sent invitations to Harding's team through several different angles. He was not successful in his attempts to lure presidential hopeful Warren G. Harding, twenty-ninth president of the United States. That didn't matter to Carl Fisher, if a plan didn't unfold as he desired, in true business fashion he unfolded the plan.

As the good people of Miami waited patiently for Harding to show up at their prepared gala in the big city across the bay, Fisher made his move. As President Elect Harding's boat arrived in Miami, Carl Fisher appeared, seemingly out of nowhere, and charmed Harding on board Fisher's boat. (Redford 1970.) Ahhh.... let the games begin.

Fisher was famously a lot of fun. He was an expert at making people comfortable and showing them a good time. In times of need, he was generally packing a couple of good cigars, good drinks and happy smiling folks- always setting the scene for enjoyment. He swept Harding to the beach to show him the tremendous development and the newest grand hotel-his Flamingo. The eleven-story hotel had a penthouse right on the bay that would show the candidate for president the view of the fabulous city he came to attend. When they got to the Flamingo Hotel the itty-bitty tour turned into, oh... look at that... a poker game waiting in the penthouse. And the players were important people, too. And, oh, my... Scotch... mmm, good Scotch at that. No one would tell. Prohibition, snowhabition, they sat down for a game and some sauce.

The next morning when Harding woke up from his restful sleep at the

Flamingo, they partook in a lively game of golf where the famous photo shoot took place. President Harding enjoyed a round of golf with Rosie, the three-year-old circus elephant as his caddy. The snapshots were rampant, the smiles abundant and the publicity was all free. Just as Carl had planned.

Ahhh... the power of a golf course.

A few years later, Rosie became even more famous. Carl Fisher wrote a friend saying, "450 Hoosier Shriners called on me this morning at 8:30, and with proper ceremonies they made 'Rosie', my pet elephant a member of the Shrine, being the only female in the world a real Shrine member. How's that for publicity?" (Fisher Papers 1928.)

At the time, the golf course was the focal point from the windows of Carl Fisher's Lincoln Hotel. The area was empty and peaceful. Cars were few and visitors enjoyed the soft ocean breeze and inviting waters. Hustle and bustle didn't exist on the beach then, instead the tone was relaxed.

Even with the new addition on the Lincoln Hotel, the hotel guestbook was filled and difficult to get reservations. Fisher was the comparative Donald Trump of his day. He wanted the best for his guests for one reason.

It was the best.

When people decided to visit a destination of Carl Fisher's they knew they were in for a good time, first-class treatment and a restful, magnificent, stay. Fisher opened up Broad Ripple Farm to serve his guests properly. Located near Prairie Avenue just north of 41st Street, the farm was to supply guests with butter, cream and milk – spectacular treats back in the early 19th century. Later a couple of pigs, vegetables and sugar cane added to the collection of 40 guernsey cows. The decorations that adorned the hotel were extravagant, elegant and classy. It was the best, nothing but the best. In all of Miami and Miami Beach, the Lincoln Hotel's rates were double that of the best hotels. (Kleinberg 1989, 117.)

The electricity from the Miami Beach Electric Company to the Lincoln Hotel wasn't right for Carl. The current wasn't steady, proved unreliable and didn't satisfy Fisher's level of quality. As a result, Fisher built The Miami Beach Electric Company, on Terminal Island (near Fisher Island at Government Cut). The electricity from Fisher's company lit the Lincoln Hotel starting on December 13, 1920. On December 21, seventy huge electrical lights lit up Lincoln Road.

While Fisher was putting the finishing touches on The Lincoln Hotel's interior, his generosity was clear. According to Jane, Carl's wife, he was stressed from being stretched too thin financially and went for a walk up Lincoln Road. He encountered an old man with a wagon outside the Lincoln Hotel where some of the hotel's furnishings sat waiting for installation. Fisher happened upon the man struggling to load the heavy bathtub into his wagon. When Carl asked what he was doing, the answer was blunt. The old man said he was taking the bathtub because no one needed as much money as that Carl Fisher guy and he needed a bathtub. Fisher didn't introduce himself as he helped the man load the tub as well as some of the other items. (Fisher 1947.)

Shortly after the hotel was completed the land boom hit the area. Shady business dealers were making their moves by pushing paper, overpricing sales and often selling unfit land at severely inflated prices. They often used Carl Fisher's name in their dealings as weight for their sale.

This didn't please Fisher at all. In addition, gambling was taking a stronghold on the beach; women showed up hunting for a sugar daddy, and more importantly, **Al Capone** and his henchmen impregnated the beach with an unappealing element. To make matters worse the government made alcohol illegal with the enactment of **Prohibition**. Carl Fisher, like most of us, didn't like being told what to do by government officials so when Prohibition hit the law books, Fisher started drinking.

Take all these factors and ball them into Fisher's financial stresses that were growing from the falling economy… boom! Together they created a fireball. Fisher was not happy with some of the riffraff setting up shop on his beach. He was adamant about enforcing the laws so that the area could remain safe for families. His anguish turned into political pressure. He succumbed to the only retaliation he knew, he climbed on the Mayer's back to make sure the police force was doing their duty.

One sleepless night, Carl felt led to do his own checking on the local misdoings. More specifically he was checking on the ineffective and questionable police force. He left his home at the ocean, walked up Lincoln Road and snuck around to the garden area of the Lincoln Hotel to peek in the windows, checking on the police presence. As he was peeping from window to window he was surprised by a policeman who without delay arrested Fisher as a Peeping Tom. The officer was new and didn't know Fisher, so he followed protocol and took the lawbreaking trespasser down to jail.

The Lincoln Hotel was the first of many hotels built by Carl Fisher. He chose to build his hotels on land that was more economical for a purpose. This left the most valuable ocean front property for potential buyers. Fisher's whole plan for his hotels was to create a relaxing atmosphere where his customers could slow down and take in the beauty of Miami Beach. He wanted them comfortable with hopes that they would then buy a lot of their own.

Towards the end of The Great Depression, business prices became volatile and all hotel business was ailing. The Lincoln Hotel rates dropped from $40.00 per night to $5.49. (Kleinberg 1994.)

After Carl Fisher died, a New York developer bought the building, took it down to the ground and rebuilt the **Mercantile Building** now known as **420 Lincoln Road**. The building now humbly resides on the National Register of Historic Places as it contains monumental historic value. Stepping into the building reveals elaborate **murals** done by Leo Birchansky in 1945. (Root 1987.) Murals made their mark during this timeframe, setting the stage for the comeback of Lincoln Road. Murals are like the Art Deco buildings as they depict a time in history. The Great Depression caused a lot of lost jobs, especially for the creative sector. The government ingeniously found ways to put these people to work; one method was with hiring artists to paint murals. Murals tell a story both of the time frame and historically. "Artists and writers were hired by the Works Progress Administration. Most of the murals in public buildings were commissioned by the U.S. Treasury Department's Section of Painting and Sculpture." (Root 1987.)

The Mercantile National Bank Building became home base for the Florida Power & Light Company. The new owner morphed into the son of the New York developer. The son morphed into the new mayor of Miami Beach. Mayor Uberman was known for telling the fellow councilmen his famous quip, "I move we abdicate for the day. I got work to do."(Kleinberg 1994.)

As you continue the walking tour, you can use the black marble you see here as a mental comparison between marble and terrazzo. **Terrazzo** was commonly used in building Art Deco style. Terrazzo floors are made up of marble chips strategically placed in cement either in patterns to form a picture or haphazardly. The terrazzo can tell a story or just add ambiance to a location. However you cut it, it was a versatile product that proved economical and extremely versatile. In some hotels terrazzo floors are used to direct guests in a certain direction while a martini glass designed in the floor shows where the bar is located. Terrazzo goes hand in hand with murals as the two represent a time of restructuring and use art form to tell history.

The Mercantile Building is often occupied by law offices.

The sea grape comes in countless moldable forms and tolerates salt air well. See the visitor?

How about now?

In the center grass median you'll find some of the most intriguing trees of the area. The trees on showcase on this island of grass are staples to the South Florida climate. Currently, aerial roots are beginning to form. The **Banyans and Stranglers**, a.k.a. fig or ficus, develop aerial roots that stretch down to the ground as the tree grows. These famous tropical trees are intermixed with the Sea Grape tree that yes, grows edible grapes. The Sea Grape was a staple to the Native American Indians that were the first residents of Southern Florida.

The Banyan trees are members of the Mulberry family, with over 1,000 different varieties. They often start in a non-traditional manner. Frequently birds eat the luscious fruit and drop the seeds. The processed missiles seek any habitable location to begin new growth like the cracks of bridges or the top crowns of palm trees. The growth starts often as a strangling vine but eventually drowns out the host tree's shade and food, eventually engulfing the parent tree. What originates as other trees evolves into a banyan. As a traditionally propagated tree they start from the ground forming their massive trunk system and eventually grow the aerial roots.

The strangler vine has been compared to a boa constrictor.

The banyan strangler is drowning out and engulfing the palm on Pine Tree Drive just before 41st St.

Although these trees took a good beating during the hurricane season of 2005 when Katrina and Rita did their share of damage it was Hurricane Wilma that took out nearly half their girth.

In the South Pacific the natives have tied aerial roots together to form living bridges. Calcutta is known for growing the largest tree on record. The Guinness Book of World Records for 1985 describes the tree as containing 1,000 prop roots making up a tree that covered four acres.

Landscape borders represent cresting waves.

An advanced banyan.

Chapter 5
Cross Over Drexel Avenue

Curving straight lines are an oxymoron in most circles but not on Lincoln Road.

The first building on your left, on the south side of the road is the only remaining original structure on Lincoln Road. The tall office building which houses the Van Dyke Café a few blocks down runs in second place on the historical timeline. It was built four years after the church.

The Community Church at **1620 Drexel Avenue** was built in 1921 and was designed by Walter DeGarmo as the first church to preach the beach. DeGarmo came to the area with his family back in 1903 where they lived in Coconut Grove- the only major settlement of the area at the time. He was well known for the structures he designed in The Grove.

The perimeter wall is not original to the structure.

The church was a central meeting point after the devastating hurricane of 1926. At the time, hurricanes were not named which caused this storm to be known by The Hurricane, The **1926 Miami Hurricane**, The Great Miami Hurricane and even Big Blow. Miami Beach encountered a 15-foot storm surge and heavy winds estimating a Category 4 or 5 hurricane. Three feet of sand was covering the streets in spots drifting in some areas and void in others. People toughed out the storm but when the winds stopped they ventured out into the streets to check on their neighbors and assess the damage.

This was arguably the biggest mistake of Miami's history. As people walked around, they didn't realize this was the eye of the storm passing directly over Miami Beach. The eye was so large one pioneer recalled getting five blocks from her house when the second wave of wind overtook her in the middle of the street. Many residents were making their way across the connector bridges to vacate the island when the calm eye changed instantly to gusting winds as the back end of the storm hit. Over 200 people died in the storm, the population of the beach hovered around 3,000 residents at the time. In comparison, if the same size storm hit today, the damage would roughly equal a trillion dollars.

Most structures at the time, were built with materials available from salvaged ships, with a resulting inability to withstand the beating. Miami Beach felt a foretaste of the Great Depression after the 1926 storm, the remainder of the country followed in 1929. On the positive side, the storm instigated building codes and inspections that have save thousands of lives and countless dollars in damage from storms that followed. Many other cities across the nation followed suit with their own building guidelines and codes.

When The Hurricane struck, the University of Miami was on the crest of opening its doors for the first time. The school commenced its first class a few days after the storm; their nickname became The Miami Hurricanes.

The church is famous from the storm first of all because it survived, but also because during the chaos the church housed lost and orphaned children.

The church is famous for Easter egg hunts and a Halloween night of fun. *Photo courtesy of the Miami Beach Community Church.*

The history of the church goes back to 1917 where a **congregation** began to form in the little populated area. Originally, thirty-five people met at the local casino but the numbers died out quickly to a nonexistent attendance only one year later. In 1919 the Secretary of the Church Building Society of Congregational Churches of America, Reverend Luman H. Royce, came down from New York and met nine hopeful churchgoers with the intention of forming a steady congregation. Home meetings grew into a small body of less than 40 when the following year Royce met with Carl Fisher and orchestrated the donation of three properties for the church building. (Kleinberg 1994, 64-65.) The Fishers were not regular attendees of church but they believed in giving. The building was a combined effort from the sponsor church, the Fisher's, and local donations.

In Jane Fisher's book, *Fabulous Hoosier*, she tells an altered version of the tale. Jane is not shy with describing Carl as a brash man who swore like a sailor and carried a gruff and curt demeanor. She, on the other hand, was sweet and hospitable making the town a better place for all. She described their walk one day where she pleaded in her soft, delicate, demure way to build a church for the good of the people. According to Jane, Carl was abrupt and harsh with her and finally he succumbed by piercing his walking stick into the ground claiming, "Here's your G... D... church." Hence, designating that spot as the location for the church along with $50,000 for the building costs. According to Jane this gave the code name GD Church to the site. (Fisher 1947.)

The first Miami Beach Congregational Church service was officially held with the 38 parishioners at the Eunice Martin School on January 4, 1920. (Lavender 2002, 144.)

The church officially, opened with no hired pastor to lead regular services, instead visiting church leaders preached until nine months later when Reverend Elisha A. King appeared and led service until 1940. (Kleinberg 1994, 64.)

The Marielitos hit the church and countless shops on The Mall hard with the crime wave in the '80s. "Thieves kicked in the doors to the Community Church one night and stole the audio equipment used to tape Sunday sermons for shut-ins. The organ was vandalized. Someone stole the solid brass bell that summoned parishioners to services. Even the Bibles vanished." (Stofik 2005, 133.)

The current pastor, a strong voice for the homosexual community, embraces accepting any and all people no matter who they are or what their beliefs. Originally the church was built to house many different denominations with the flexibility to entertain various beliefs. The order is filled.

According to head model booker Monica Valiati, the back area of the church, entrance off Drexel, is currently being used by one of the oldest modeling agencies on the beach – paradoxical in true South Beach form.

10 am services incorporate open arms to all beliefs and alternative lifestyles.

Just past the church you'll notice a beautiful **pink flamingo**. This is one of many pink flamingos that stalk our little city with flair and life. Back a few years, the project was orchestrated by the City of Miami Beach, Art in Public Places. The goal was to liven up the joint with a little art. A naked flamingo, made of fiberglass could be purchased and then painted for display. The fiberglass flamingoes descended upon our fine city with a display of flavor for a resounding successful seven months. The project was originally planned to cover a two-month display, response was so favorable the presentation was extended. Several of the flamingoes remain to brighten up faces and pose for photo shoots by either an individual or a business. This bird was donated by the city of Miami Beach to the Latin Chamber of Commerce, which stands as a supplementary welcome center open to the public behind the church. The Latin population fills a dominating eighty percent of the work force that supports our local hotels in the service industry. This flamingo is reflective of the dynamic affect the Latino flavor holds in Miami Beach. The pink paint, donated by Richard May of Giant Motors, clothed the bird, then paint by cartoonist Rolly Oliva covered her, followed by a sheer outer shell, again by Giant Motors. Since it is covered in auto paint, the Latin Chamber proudly jokes, "It came out like a brand new chevy." (Calvani 2006.)

Rolly Oliva, famous Hanna Barbara cartoonist, donated his art skills when he moved from California to Miami.

Other cities that have done projects like this had seen great success, one used cows while another used bulls. Standard protocol is to hire the company that specializes in the project. Located in Switzerland and costing more than desired, the committee took on the job themselves.

Initially, the project was to be larger, covering more ground including the whole county. A fabricator was contacted and plans were initiated to manufacture flamingos. The Twin Towers in New York City were struck in the beginning stages of the project when a contract had not yet

been signed. It didn't seem appropriate to continue with the flamingos so the city decided to bail but since the fabricator had already made 100 of the enormous birds it flew anyway. Since no contract had been signed at that point, they downsized the project to two areas, Coral Gables and Miami Beach.

Today the project packs a punch. They symbolize art, standing on your word, and September 11th. They symbolize life and beauty after September 11th, and they symbolize the city making the city better. Most importantly, the flamingo project symbolizes standing on your own two… uh… one foot. Salute city guys! I raise my glass to you.

At **525 Lincoln Road**, is an Italian Restaurant called **Rosinella**. Years ago three brothers came across the pond to America. They opened Sport Café on 5th and Washington. Later, their mother came over from Rome and Rosinella's has been a success on Lincoln Road ever since. The family is a team that functions as one. They are humble working class people from Rome that came to America to earn a living.

This was the place to be on Lincoln Road when the Italian soccer team competed victoriously for the World Cup in 2006. The volume was high and the walls shook with each scored goal. It's important to know, the restaurant directly across from them on Lincoln Road is, of course, a French restaurant. The final match in the World Cup of 2006 was between the French and the Italians. The area contained a bit of competition at that time with one side of the street exploding with each victorious goal. It was a modern cheer of "Less filling!" and "Tastes great!" erupting from either side of Lincoln Road with each score.

The ultimate victory for the Italians seamed to be when Rosinella's draped an enormous Italian flag from the roof of their building. The flag boldly covered the two-story façade of the building overpowering the small area with "THE ITALIANS HAVE WON!" in a discreet and proper manner. This huge, consuming flag was the view for the dining French for days.

The rival, yet complementing, Italian restaurant is **Hosteria Romana** located at **429 Espanola Way** a few streets south. Flavor doesn't only encompass the eats; it embraces an attitude of home. Restaurants like these – too good and too close – create the concept of a progressive dinner on South Beach. One joint for the appetizer, one for the soup, one for the meal, one for the dessert and one for the wine. Although the meal is then extended to reach hours of enjoyment, the progressive dinner spreads the love. It also enables mingling couples to choose their preferred restaurant for their course of the meal. This American tradition of the progressive dinner usually held in communities across the country bringing neighbors closer, takes a more sophisticated flare on South Beach.

The Lincoln Theatre.

A couple of doors further to the west is the famed **Lincoln Theatre** at **555 Lincoln Road**. The Lincoln Theatre was designed in 1935 by the acclaimed architect Thomas W. Lamb along with Robert E. Collins and opened in 1936.

Now housing **The New World Symphony**, the theater is considered a masterpiece of Art Deco architecture. The façade was a jewel of dominating pink while the interior was one of the most elaborate of all the theaters.

According to his family, Lamb designed over 300 theaters worldwide with a heavy presence in New York, Pennsylvania, and Ohio. Lamb was described as a character and compared to Frank Lloyd Wright in his genius and unique personality. At a time when laughter and enjoyment was not commonplace, Lamb took a stance. Thomas W. Lamb II, Thomas Lamb's Great Grandson, said, "The wonder of his theatres came from his belief that such places might be the only experience of luxury that common folk would have. He traveled to Persia, Africa and the Mediterranean for ideas."

The Lincoln projected entertainment. Local resident Justo Varela said, "I saw The Godfather when it first came out for $1.50 at the Lincoln Theatre. It was big. It was great!"

Thomas Lamb designed over 300 theaters across the globe including the Lincoln.

Among others, Lamb was hired by Fox, Trans-Lux, Loews and Keith. His movie theatres blanketed the country. His payments for the Fox theatres were not completely traditional for the time according to his Great Grandson, "He was paid in stock for the most part which became nearly worthless when the depression hit. He utilized Tiffany's stained glass in the Art Deco design furnishings of many theatres." Lamb designed the Greyhound Bus Terminals during the '30s, which he chose to do in the continuing Art Deco style that he loved. Will Rogers, a great comedian, author, cowboy, and actor of the time, was a friend of Tom Lamb's as well as Carl Fisher's and spoke fondly of both upon each respective death. The thought of the barn doors thrown open to the laughter and practical jokes, cigars and antics of Carl Fisher, Tom Lamb, and Will Rogers hanging out together for a pow-wow at the beach is filled with flavor and energy.

One of Tomas Lamb's most beloved projects was an old farmhouse in Elizabethtown, New York located not far from Lake Champlain. He completely redid the simple layout so that it was unrecognizable to its original state. The house that contained over six bedrooms included the master bedroom that Lamb positioned on top of the silo structure with a staircase that led to the ground as it wound around the outside of the silo. After many years, the house was bought and turned into rooms for students at the nearby summer music camp. Isaac Perlman was among the students.

The theater's sidewalk is a popular place for venders.

The Lincoln Theatre was known for the unveiling of the famous movie picture, *Stagecoach* in 1939. Other premiers followed. Justo Valera described, "It was the place to go, especially for the movies. My cousin was the usher. That was a good job. I saw *Ben-Hur*. They had a big intermission so you could take a break. You got all dressed up, it was the place to be."

Recently, it was used for the unveiling of the new ***Miami Vice*** remake starring Jamie Foxx and Colin Farrell as Crockett and Tubbs. The premier included famous local celebrity guests like Hulk Hogan, Gloria Estephan, and Niki Hilton. Tickets went for roughly $250.00 a seat but the real buzz was outside where spectators were packed tight and deep like pickles in packing juice hoping to see the famous actors attending the showing. Both lead characters were not in attendance.

The Lincoln Theatre is a famous historic destination complete with concerts and premiers.

In the glory days, The Lincoln was filled with stylish Art Deco fixtures including a terrazzo entryway that made up the lobby area. The sloped floor is blamed as a slippery encounter that proved hazardous for many and even accused as the reason for the final death of the theater. The last days were filled with $1 movies and sadly molded seats. When you walked into the theatre it smelled. Not only did it smell, but when you left, the odor clung to you like a ripe sock. Guests turned into human transporters, moving the disgusting odor around town like a cheap rancid perfume. Some could withstand the cloud of funk but those with sensitive noses didn't dare enter.

The Lincoln Road Mall had successfully made the transformation from an active high-end shopping zone of the '50s to a ghost town in the '80s. Locals repeatedly comment that when the symphony came in 1987, you could roll a bowling ball down the middle of Lincoln Road and not hit a thing.

As Lincoln Road declined in popularity, the theater entered a state of confusion. It was once popular and beautiful but had turned into an undesired smelly has-been. The Lincoln Theatre was a beautiful place trapped in a location that was dead to pedestrians at the time. Still, if you looked really hard, it showed a glimmer of potential.

At that time, in 1987, Conductor Michael Tilson Thomas dreamed of an orchestra that taught and trained new musicians. This was a dream that appeared impossible until Ted Arison, of the Carnival Cruise Line, came on the scene and changed history as well as Lincoln Road. Various musicians from around the country were hand chosen to make up and form the now coveted symphony.

The theater incorporates Art Deco style with window eyebrows.

The Plymouth Hotel on 21st Street was bought as housing quarters. At the time the hotel was tired and worn down but still loved and used by the elderly residents that called the building home. The price and location was right for the new musicians' housing quarters. The seniors were asked to leave but given a fluffy departure time because of their ages. As the new students to the symphony moved in the elderly residents greeted them with smiles and welcoming hugs. The seniors helped them move in their boxes and instruments. The older crowd mingled with the younger generation to the point were cookouts and card games filled the air along with the practicing instruments.

Nearly a million dollars updated the interior. Old smelly seats were ripped out, walls were redone, fixtures were updated, and love was painted on the solid walls. The theater seats 713 with a performing stage of over 2000 square feet. The aura of the theater is only topped by the exceptional acoustics.

Across the mall from the Lincoln Theatre is **Cafeteria** located at **546 Lincoln Road**. This restaurant was brought down from New York and has become a popular scene especially with the locals. They're known for being open twenty-four hours a day, seven days a week, as well as serving breakfast all the way up to 6 pm. Their rooftop lounge, appropriately named Air, is notoriously Zen with flowing aura and slate rock bar that doubles as a waterfall.

Originally, the building was a **Cadillac dealership** with the new fangled horseless carriage filling the showroom floor. The insignia above the door shows the later car models sold at the dealership. The LaSalle was a popular model made by General Motors during the Art Deco revolution that was changing worldwide history. Sadly, the LaSalle line was cancelled once it continually overshadowed the Cadillac sales numbers. The Cadillac was not only the parent car to the automobile manufacturer; it was the older auto body as well as the more expensive car.

Cafeteria started off as a car dealership for the early Cadillac models.

Charles F. Kettering, inventor of the self-starter was a good friend of Carl Fisher's. They were nearly neighbors up north. Fisher lived in Indianapolis changing automobile history with the headlight. Kettering lived just outside of Dayton inventing and perfecting multiple aspects of the automobile including the diesel engine. Many trips were made back and forth to each man's town. Kettering's small town now bears his name, Kettering, Ohio. The self-starter was originally an optional feature for the Cadillac models of 1911. By the 1920s, the self-starter was coming standard issue making crank starts obsolete. These are the cars that were featured behind these large display windows. Size for size, comparing today's car with the displayed models behind these windows, the show models took up roughly the space of a Mini Cooper, much smaller than our auto beasts of today.

But onto more important things, what exactly are the rhythmically positioned **shiny screws in the sidewalk**? Theses patterned buttons are anchor bolts for flying buttress braces that hold up protective metal plates. The metal plates cover the bottom few feet of the large windows during hurricanes.

The garage door to the car service area is now home to an ATM machine.

Chapter 6
Cross Over Pennsylvania Avenue

The Sony Music Building is on the market for $12 million.

On the north side of Lincoln Road is the famous **Sony Building** at **605 Lincoln.** And is that ... ? ... Why yes... I do believe it is yet another **Starbucks**. This is the latest and third Starbucks on Lincoln Road, but oh, I see, it's different. It has music. You can buy individual songs to make up your perfect CD and pay only for what you purchase.

One of Starbuck's goals is to never have a customer wait in line for coffee. It appears they are meeting this goal with multiple outlets. While you're here in America's subtropical paradise, request the Bahamian's tropical version of a cup of coffee. You won't find it on the menu here so you have to ask: subtract the cream and sugar and add a hearty wedge of lime.

This location for Sony Music is important since this is the Latino capital of America. This Sony is the Sony Music Latino Division. The MTV Latino Network began their broadcast here in 1993 with twenty-two Spanish-speaking countries receiving the feed with giddy anticipation. MTV Latino quickly grew into one of Latin

America's favorite channels. This comes as no shock as Latin America is known for their mesmerizing dance steps accompanied by high-energy toned dancers. It's the way of life for most Latinos where toe tapping is near blasphemy but dancing is life.

Back on The Mall, it's easy to see the lack of public benches. At the time of design, the area was filled to overflowing with elderly. It was quiet, slow and peaceful. The elderly were intermixed with a large number of international vacationers, the lifeblood of the stores. The merchants didn't want to encourage the loitering of the elderly who needed a spot to rest their weary legs. Lapidus designed many shade inviting opportunities for a cooling moment of relief. This was a welcome and hateful concept rolled into one. The hope was to lead the elderly to restaurants where they would sit and order something to cool their throats instead of simply sitting under a projected art form for the day.

Lapidus said, "My feeling of architecture has nothing to do with stone and mortar and marble. It has something to do with the human soul." He wanted a working project with the variety of desires from merchants as well as the needs of shoppers. His technique was different from anything else presented at the time. The people who viewed his work loved it but ironically it wasn't taken well by his fellow architects who ostracized and demeaned his new designs. Upon his death, Lapidus was responsible for designing 1,200 buildings and 250 hotels across the globe. His work was more of a dynamic thunderstorm than an easy rain. His peers and critics discharged his new style as vulgar and offensive. The people loved his style but the architectural community abhorred it and was not shy on their vocal expressions. Lapidus himself said, "The critics hated my work – but the people love it." (Obituary on the AP wire)

Lapidus designed much of Miami Beach including popular locations like the Di Lido, Biltmore Terrace, Algiers, and the Sans Souci to mention only a handful. These monumental projects were nothing in comparison to his next request to design the Fontainebleau immediately chased by the Eden Roc.

Shortly afterwards came the Lincoln Road project. It was perfect for Lapidus as he was skilled in the retail sector. As a young architect, strait from school at the Columbia University School of Architecture, Lapidus began his career working in his field but moonlighting with work designing retail stores. This was not his love; he desired to create buildings that would change skylines across the world not shopping malls, but he needed the money. Lapidus had a rare skill that proved favorable with the retail sector. When he was hired for a project, he didn't just build what he wanted; he first studied the project. He observed what was needed both by the business sector occupying the space and the people attending the space. He watched human patterns, human desires and then designed the project to fit the need. This is the talent that made him so famous. Even though he didn't long to design blueprints for shopping areas for his life work, has was making more money moonlighting than with planning buildings. Lapidus said, "In my store work I was purely interested in commerce. The goal was to grab a customer walking down the street and say, come in – I've got something to show you."

He didn't like working with the stores, but it made money so he took on the jobs. Lapidus told *Metropolis Magazine*, "I had studied architecture, and stores were not architecture. The stores depend on brilliant light, the use of color, and one other thing I noticed: people do not make a beeline for the thing they want to buy. They meander. So I shaped the walls in unusual forms. My whole concept of life is to make it more unusual, more interesting, more warm."(Ringen 2001.)

Lapidus knew how to perform for the people who hired him. Again, he looked at what was needed, studied how people acted and then made his designs to match the needs of the people. But he didn't stop there. He took it a step further and designed unspoken desires. This was evident when he planned the coat check, stairway-to-nowhere, at the Fontainebleau. Lapidus told *Metropolis Magazine*, "Then when I got into hotels, I had to rethink, what am I selling now? You're selling a good time." He took that idea and ran with it.

Still, his enemy was his own peers. "The critics bashed his style." He was described as "gaudy kitsch." The reality and depth of hatred was fully understood when Lapidus was attending a meeting at the Americana, a hotel in Miami Beach designed by Lapidus. The meeting was filled with popular architects of the day for 1963. Other architects affronted Lapidus and hurled insults at him on his style and design. Rude is too nice a word to describe the treatment Lapidus received. Sadly, this was not a one-stop encounter for him. The hatred

Morris Lapidus used geometric shapes to extend design while balancing the visual weight of a structure.

ran deep from his critics and peers. (Obituary on the AP wire)

The *New York Times* termed his work as, "superschlock. Pornography of architecture, sniffed *Art in America*." *The Miami Herald* joked about Lapidus designs in a hateful manner when they said, "it was probably not too disturbing to people who have lost their eyesight." Morris Lapidus was deeply affected by these hurtful critics, yet he was continually hired to produce more of the same.

Miami Beach 411 said, "His obsession with detail extended to bellboys' uniforms, done in purple with gold braid. The critic Anna Louise Huxtable memorably described them as looking 'like an exploding eggplant'." Critics weren't just evaluating and stamping an opinion on Lapidus' work, they were pulverizing him and his designs, grinding him to a fine powder with revulsion.

It affected Morris Lapidus, rightfully so, as he had ears to hear and a brain to process the unrelenting free flowing faucet of disgust. He is quoted at *Miami Beach 411* as saying, "The critics, they just not only didn't like my work, they couldn't say enough horrible things about me. I was never published for over thirty years in any architectural book or magazine. I was anathema." For any man to consider himself abhorred and an abomination is about as deep as hatred can come.

"By 1985, when critics still didn't appreciate his work, he folded up his office and said to hell with it. It took two large trucks to consign all the materials to the flames, he wrote in his autobiography *Too Much is Never Enough*. He had billed $50 million during his career, and should have realized that this sum was the surest mark of appreciation in the land of the American Dream." (Obituary on the AP wire) The money didn't fully do it for Lapidus, proving in a way, the power of the tongue. Lapidus held a private bonfire filled with his life's paperwork and passion.

His work here on Lincoln Road is a nontraditional shopping mall, not his passion. Regardless, it was what he knew and they hired him, so he performed. *Miami Beach 411* said, "Lapidus was one of the first to create storefronts with wide glass facades through which customers could view the actual store. His designs eliminated the system where clerks stood behind counters guarding the merchandise, instead allowing customers to wander and handle the goods." This process of design was used in nearly every shopping venue in the country by that time. Lapidus set the pace.

When Morris Lapidus died at the age of ninety-eight he only had a few short years of appreciation to absorb. He was honored by the Smithsonian Institution in New York as well as the City of Miami Beach and also by The Miami Design Preservation League.

A plaque and dedication ceremony was made to him here on Lincoln Road, at the Euclid Pavilion where the brass plaque still hangs today. He saw these few minor accolades before he died on January 18, 2001. Morris Lapidus was a hard working Russian immigrant who was well hired for his work but thoroughly criticized by educated people with blinders infected with "tunnel thinking." Today the architectural community sees Lapidus with more accolades. His life made a mark on the world as well as the classroom for future architects and artists. He didn't see the hundreds of architect students who continue to study his work. He didn't see the younger generation of architects receive commissions to restore buildings Lapidus designed. This is perceived as one of the most honored requests in the architectural community. In the end, Lapidus paid a price for his designs, teaching us all a lesson.

As you walk along you'll notice the sidewalk comes in various colors and patterns. This is done by design. "Lapidus took cues from the vibrant paving patterns of the broad promenades along Ipanema and Copacana beaches in Rio de Jeneiro. He envisioned black-and-white-striped pavement stretching the entire width of the right-of-way from building face, but budgetary constraints limited him."(Nash 2004.) If you look closely, you'll see where the budget allowed for the filling in of the street, leaving the original sidewalks from 1920. This allows you to walk right where Carl Fisher walked, stepping all over the man's dream and making a fulfilled victory.

Water was an integral aspect of the Morris Lapidus design.

At **625 Lincoln Road**, you'll find the local favorite: **Zeke's.** This is a bar that sells beer. Imagine that! What makes Zeke's special is any beer, any time, no matter what label or where the import, each for $3.00. Yes, $3.00 for a Corona and even $3.00 for a St. Paulie's Girl. All bottles, all $3.00. There's no waitress so just grab a table, grab a beer and grab a dose of relax. They'll never make you feel rushed at Zeke's where everyone's a local.

This is a much different atmosphere than the years past when during the celebration of Lincoln Road's 70th birthday in 1975, this spot was flooded with bubbly pink champagne, free for all from Sandra Post.

Gelateria Parmalat, located at **670 Lincoln Road** is home to Italian import gelato. Here they make the frosty treat daily. The Travel Channel showcased the frosty spot as the, "Best see and be seen spot in Miami Beach." In addition, Rachael Ray ate a mid-day snack here, on camera, when she brought her show "$40.00 A Day" on Food Network, to South Beach.

When you ask a local, the store will design any style cake you wish, made entirely of gelato. They can make any cake for any occasion and do it perfectly to your specifications while mixing, matching, and layering to your specific desires. This is not done anywhere else. The store is no dollar-a-cup ice cream joint, it's more of a savor every bite kind of treat.

Chapter 7
Cross Over Euclid Avenue

Right in the center of The Mall is one of the most well-known and recognizable meeting places on the road. The **Euclid grass island** is also one of the only spots to sit. Sadly, that makes it a place for drunken vagrants, but it also makes it a great place for the kids to watch the balloon twisting man.

The whole area of the grass island is complete in design. The mere existence of the island creates the unrelenting feel that a concert is about to commence. The air buzzes with celebration at this spot, even at six in the morning when the only visible life is a handful of street cleaners sprinkled with dedicated runners.

The Euclid pavilion is often used for comedy, concerts, Halloween costume contests, and more.

The Euclid grass island is a relaxing place to people-watch. Often the **parrots** that roost in the palms are so loud you can't speak at all but the celebration only makes the area tropically charming. I wrongly assumed these parrots were natural to the area. In zoos up north we have tropical parrots on display for viewing. My thought was, "Wow, parrots in the trees, if I go to the zoo here am I going to find Robins, Blue Jays, and Cardinals?"

Different species of parrots flock in the surrounding areas.

I have since heard these parrots *are* from the zoo. I've been told that when Hurricane Andrew blew through in 1992 the bird sanctuary was destroyed by the destructive winds. The bird pavilion took a major beating. *The Sun Sentinel* reported, "It was just a few pieces of mesh flapping in the winds where there used to be a wonderful tent of a rainforest." The majority of wild birds that took flight with the winds were captured through various channels. A state trooper found a pheasant from Asia strolling down the turnpike. The officer loaded the pheasant into the patrol car and delivered him back to the zoo, sans handcuffs he was retuned to his home behind bars with no possibility of parole. Other animals were recovered in the same manner. An antelope was walking through the administrative offices and monkeys were found scampering along Coral Reef Drive.

Now the zoo's aviary is back in flight with a new iron mesh netting stretched over the top. The new netting is designed to hold up under Category 5 winds. This, however, is not the right history for these parrots. A representative from the zoo said they didn't, and don't, have parrots, they leave that to The Parrot Jungle. The zoo speculates pet birds were freed in mass by the hurricane and have adapted to the area very well.

Foreign pets released into the general population is not an uncommon site here. Unlike the Burmese python population found in the Everglades, the parrots are not swallowing six-foot alligators whole. As far as released pets go, they are relatively harmless as well as adaptable to the area. The parrots are added to the list of exotics introduced that now thrive in our area like the pink flamingo, iguanas, and peacocks.

Parrots are native to South America, thanks to hurricanes we can embrace their song.

As for these parrots, a number of exotic birds were reported lost in Hurricane Andrew by individual dealers. These parrots appeared on Lincoln Road directly after Andrew and appear to be the **green conure parrot**. At this point some of them are descendants of the original escapees. The green conure are basically, "large parakeets native to Central and South America." They are considered the charismatic clowns of the parrot family. (Avian web.)

The green conure is known to have red coloration somewhere on his body depending on his size, gender and variety. They gather every morning and evening in their nesting spots like clockwork here on Lincoln Road.

On the corner of Lincoln Road and Euclid Avenue is a well attended restaurant, **Nexxt Café**. Usually when you see a restaurant filled with customers it's a good way to tell if the food is worth the cost and the service is exemplary. In this situation, that's not the case. Solid attendance here is the direct result of location, location, location. Better food here is found at **Pizza Rustica**.

As the history of Lincoln Road has proved a rough life consisting of high-class shopping, decline in the economy, uplift, crime, more crime and drugs. The road has not always been a profitable shopping zone. Lincoln Road has lived a full life of stress and unsettled battles between pedestrian mall versus traditional road.

A short number of years after the road was transformed to the pedestrian mall success was faint. Many storeowners were doing all they could to bring in shoppers. At that time, many storefronts wanted action. Together they petitioned the city for change by transforming the road back to a traditional street. This idea would have invited an unfathomable cost of $3.5 million. The price paid to originally transform the street was only $600,000. This idea was meager. At another point the city manager considered enclosing this section of the mall with a roof extending from here back to where you entered the official mall at Washington Avenue. Obviously the idea was never passed.

Storeowners were put in the position to wait out the dull time of vacant shops. The artists, the homosexual community, and the preservationists eventually resuscitated the area.

Most of Lapidus' designs on Lincoln Road were for tropical foliage enclosures.

At **721, Lincoln Road** you'll find **Tiramesu**, at **723 Lincoln Road** you'll find **Le Bon** and at **731 Lincoln Road** you'll find **Spris**. All three restaurants share the same owner and all share the best deal on Lincoln Road.

Every local I know is thankful to this trio for good food and a good deal- if you know how to get it. Starting at 5:30 and stretching until 7:00, you can order certain meals for certain deals. Each restaurant has a "beat the clock" menu. The deal is this, if you order your meal at 5:30, your meal is $5.30, if you order at 5:45, your meal is $5.45 and so on until 7.

Tiramesu has a pasta list to choose from, Le Bon has a list of oysters while Spris has a variety of pizza's; however, at Spris you also get a beer or soda with your meal for the "beat the clock" price.

The other pizza on the island worth spending stomach space on is way down at **437 Washington Avenue** closer to the southern tip of the island. **Fratelli La Bufala**, which as you can tell, uses the most delicious bufala cheeses that make all the difference has no comparison. Mozzareli di bufala is a well-honored and adored Italian cheese. This mozzarella is made solely from buffalo milk, specifically from one milking at dawn. If I were visiting the area with time for one meal, I would choose Fratelli La Bufala without hesitation.

Sandwiched between these beat the clock gems is *the* gay bar on South Beach. Most people credit the artists and the gays for saving Lincoln Road and South Beach. A well-known fact is publicized across America. When the gay folks move into an area the housing values go up. This is true for

Fountains on Lincoln Road provide cooling mists.

a reason; they clean up the joint. This club shows the perfect example if you hit the back alley. When you walk the dingy passageway behind the shops you'll find back doors, garbage cans, grease barrels, dumpsters and a dirty smelly street. This location is different. The paint is fresh, the staircase from the second floor is lined with flower boxes, the dumpster area is housed in a beautiful gated fence and surrounded by potted trees. It's a foliage extravaganza pleasing the eye with fresh welcoming open arms instead of... trash.

If you're lucky enough to vacation South Beach on Halloween this is the spot to come. For most people dressing up at Halloween is the best time of the year. For the regulars at Score, this is show time. Some folks spend all year and thousands of dollars on costumes. This is entertainment at its best.

Halloween lights up Lincoln Road, especially at Score.

Next to these three restaurants on Lincoln Road, you'll notice an island of landscaping. The tree on the southern portion of the island is one of the best looking specimens in Southern Florida of the crescentia cujete commonly known as the **Calabash or Sausage Fruit Tree, or Sausage Tree**.

This gorgeous tree produces flowers all year round. The pungently sweet, musky smell from the flowers is associated with fresh cabbages. The smell becomes more prominent at night for one reason, this is when the flowers bloom to attract the pollinating bats. The Sausage Tree needs

Geometric formations define Lincoln Road.

a necessary companion tree within a one-mile radius in order to grow successfully. The flowers morph into fruit known as gourds that can be formed and shaped by tying with a cord while growing. This is done if the gourd will be used as a culinary vessel after it is dried. The possibilities are endless.

Mature dried gourds contain seeds and white powdery pulp. Immature gourds are poisonous but as the fruit matures the pulp evaporates and turns into a powder. The gourds have been used medicinally to treat skin problems like acne or even snake bites. It's also been used to treat syphilis and rheumatism.

In Africa, they use the fruit to flavor beer much like we use lime to flavor Corona and is also used as a fermenting agent. In Nicaragua, they cook the seeds to make a drink while in Hawaii, they fill the dried gourds with dried seeds and use them as hula rattles. The hardwood is used for making tool handles and fuel as well as canoes.

The calabash gourd is known to reach sizes of twelve inches long by eight inches wide with a weight of fifteen pounds. The flowering cords have been known to commonly reach ten feet long. (Barwick 2004.)

At **774 Lincoln Road**, at the other end of the block, you can see the same design already seen. This was the **Chrysler Showroom** back when cars were still being introduced to America. Ironically the pedestrian mall that allows no cars used to be home to three dealerships.

Just off the corner unit used to be **Moseley's.** This is a store that more than a few of us are sad to see gone. They closed for business due to retirement in 2006 and now we'll all have to sleep on poor quality sheets from this day forth. Moseley's was famous on this spot and always did a handsome business even when the crime was at its peak and the customers were dry. The higher echelon of society knew Moseley's and flew in just for shopping trips.

They sold bed linens, bath towels and table linens of the highest thread count and quality. Specially made items were an everyday order. It was nothing for Moseley's to special order a tablecloth of the finest linen able to fit the castle's dining table no matter how long the material stretched. It was also nothing for Moseley's to see customers travel overseas for the day just to place orders from swatches.

Celebrities, Princess Grace of Monaco, and even sultans crossed the threshold that now houses a Macintosh store and clothing venue. At Moseley's it cost a good penny for an item, even when they closed for retirement, you could buy an opened bag of gift-wrap bows for $5.00. For eighty percent off that was a hefty price for standard issue Christmas bows. The only challenge with Moseley's was they always seemed to be closed. Closed for lunch. Closed for a meeting. Closed for a private showing. Closed for a back scratch. The shop was definitely not for the every day Wal-Mart junkie.

The flowers bloom at night to attract nocturnal pollinators.

The calabash tree is a vital resource in other countries.

Metal fins are definitive Art Deco.

Stepping further you'll notice the half way mark: Meridian Avenue. This is the worst cross traffic you'll find on the road. This challenge of traffic was part of the plan for designing architect Morris Lapidus but it was not followed through because of a restricted budget. Bridges humping over the roads were originally part of the design as were a lighting design representing the stars. The budget was financially responsible and the ideas were slimmed to a more conservative proposal.

If you take a right on Meridian Avenue, you'll find the locally known Chinese food haven: **Miss Yip's at 1661 Meridian Avenue**. Ahh... just the thought of Miss Yip's and my tongue is swiping my lips at the mere suggestion. This is by far, the greatest restaurant in the area if you're a Chinese food lover; it's actually bliss at the end of a chopstick.

Just past Miss Yip's on the corner of the next block is Burdine's Department Store, oops, **Macy's**. This famous chain is one of the most historical places in all of Miami. W. M. Burdine was a citrus farmer further up state when the great frost of 1895 struck his crop and froze the whole harvest. The damage was catastrophic to the oranges and pushed Burdine over the edge and into the mercantile business. He switched gears completely. Ironically, this is the same frost that brought Henry Flagler and his railroad down to Miami.

W.M. Burdine & Sons' first store opened in the city of Miami in August of 1898 right during the peak of the heat. *The Miami Metropolis*, on August 12, 1898, announced the occasion to the whole city, "Mr. W.M. Burdine will move his family (and they are most excellent people) to Miami early next week. Carpenters are now at work providing additional shelf space and one of the largest stores of dry goods, clothing and gents' furnishings ever brought to Miami is being opened up and put into place." The simple thought of a newspaper today presenting a family in that manner is unfathomable.

The orange trees are not currently seen in Miami because of the citrus ban brought on by the citrus canker. The ban was lifted in 2005 after the record-breaking hurricane season of twenty-eight named storms, seven of which were over category 3 status. The season started with Arlene on June 8, 2005 and ended with Zeta on January 6, 2006. The traditional season runs from June 1 to November 30. This unprecedented storm activity exhausted the English alphabet causing meteorologists to venture into the Greek alphabet. The citrus canker was a wind born disease. The hurricanes would have carried the disease so there was no more point to the citrus ban.

The Holocaust Museum, one block past Macy's, is open and free to the public.

Chapter 8
Cross Over Meridian Avenue

The first storefront on your left is one of the main locations for ArtCenter/**South Florida**. The artists occupy three locations on The Mall at **800, 810, and 924 Lincoln Road.** A lot of people honor ArtCenter for breathing life back into The Mall when business was strained from crime in the '80s.

With roughly 60,000 square feet of studio space many artists are able to let their talent flow. This particular location is known as the gallery, where the artists display their works. All pedestrians are welcome inside to observe the new creations. The displays are always revolving, the doors are practically always open, and admission is free. The gallery is the perfect place in paradise for viewing artwork. Further down The Mall, you'll notice the other buildings for the artists. All locations are open to the public where you can watch the artists paint or purchase artwork right on the spot. Artists are obligated to spend roughly thirty hours a week working in their rented studio. This makes the opportunity to see artists working a near hit every visit.

ArtCenter is a nonprofit entity started in 1985 to further the vocation of art, not just painting. Sadly, a few take the shock response and call it art instead of choosing to enlighten and awe. The chance of pushing the line is more frequent in a community so open to alternative lifestyles. Distracting little children's eyes is sometimes necessary. On the same note, there are some very impressive pieces.

The whole art movement in the area was started to better the district. Ellie Schneiderman originally rented the collective space with then intention to make a difference with the art world. After much hard work and perseverance the buildings were eventually purchased through grants totaling over $60,000 and assistance. ArtCenter is crowned and honored with the claim of saving Lincoln Road. At that time, in 1985, over a hundred vacancies existed in the stores on Lincoln Road. Even a few years later, more than a quarter of the shops were vacant with the greatest number of vacancies near the west end of the road. Artists brought in people, even if it was just the artists themselves to start, the live bodies were a necessity on the road. Plenty of rentable apartments surrounded the area giving the artists the availability to stay close to their worksites and spend quality time developing their skills.

Art Center South Florida is free and open to the public.

The massive sea of square footage was leased at less than a quarter the price of other spaces. Another storefront was filled with an art supply distributor rounding out the situation. This was the perfect peg for the hole because it not only met the needs of the artists but also filled one of the amply vacant properties. The ghost town road was seeing life. Not just strung-out life, jonesin' for an evening toke or criminal life wondering if they should rob the same store again or hit a new one for the evening. This life was making a difference.

This mass vacancy was realistically a combination of factors including the crime in the 1980s, the opening of Disney World in 1970, and the opening of suburban malls in the 1960s. Collectively they pulled people away from the area. Visitors stayed away by the millions. In truth, it was mostly the crime that held advancement at bay.

Almost every store had problems with burglars, only the restaurants were spared. One shop owner put up a sign explaining the furs were made of fake materials to deter vandals and theft. Criminals became bold as they found the police force couldn't equal the crime threat. Some took their time and unloaded merchandise for hours.

The Herald held a whole page for the store owners to have their say in the Living Today section back in October of 1980. The Duty Free Shop at 901 experienced the pain, "They smashed his windows 13 times. He can't even get insurance anymore. It's a sad deal." The store had only been in business 11 months at the time. (Browning 1980.)

Countless windows were smashed, with a price of nearly $1,000 each. Many owners settled on the ugly option of permanently boarding up their windows. *The Herald* quoted another unspecified storeowner, "After the eighth smash-in our insurance dropped us." Surprisingly, it wasn't all the Marielitos. The paper reported, "Everybody robs us. Once it was three black youths. Once it was four Puerto Rican kids. Once it was a woman with two guys. It's not just refugees." (Browning 1980.)

Storeowners were left with little choices. One businessman told the paper the thieves had already taken over $50,000 in product from him through several robberies. He opted to sleep in his store, on the balcony, with a prepared 12-guage Remington. (Browning 1980.)

The Marielitos came to America when the communist government took over Cuba in 1959. Then again flooded our port in 1980 when Fidel Castro opened his prisons allowing captives, as well as free people to leave Cuba in the Mariel Boatlift. Cubans today say the way to leave Cuba through Mariel was if you were a criminal or if you told them you were a homosexual.

The group was mixed. Some were criminal; most were regular citizens seeking freedom. "According to Immigration and Naturalization Service (INS) figures, a total of 1,700 persons representing 1.4% of the new emigrants, were classified as felons (convicted of murder, rape or burglary). (Silva 1985.) Over 250,000 Cubans came during the boatlift.

A buzz was created from the volume of people hitting the area. Criminals broke into stores and started a domino effect of rampant crime. The same way a riot instills the crazy gene in law-abiding citizens, the Marielito's arrival awakened crime. For the Marielitos there was little comparison to crimes committed in America. Most Cuban immigrants will tell you it is illegal to buy groceries from any location other than a government store in Cuba. But if you do something the government doesn't like, for example applying for a visa to America, they remove your right to shop in a government store. Black market groceries are a staple for survival. The government arrests almost anyone at any time if they like. This is done by design. When the port of Mariel was opened, hard-core criminals were released but regular folks looking to feed their families were also released.

When the Marielitos hit land in South Florida, crime increased uncontrollably. The statistics on this are real. This was a dangerous area to live. You didn't go out at night, you didn't go anywhere alone, you put bars on your windows, and you crossed the street at any sign of lurking danger.

One senior told me a few Marielitos broke into her apartment through the back kitchen door. She and her husband were watching "Murder She Wrote" on television. The robbers went right to the bedroom and took everything they had of value while the elderly couple sat terrified with fright. From that day on, including today, her back door has been nailed shut and her drapes remain closed. The apartment is on the second floor with no back stairwell.

A great portion of Miamians credit the **artists** with saving the area from the rampant crime. A couple of the first artists who came to develop their skills began the resuscitation of Lincoln Road. They set up a movie screen in the middle of the pedestrian mall, sold popcorn and ran silent movies one day each week. A piano player accompanied the silent movies and collected tips. This started the trend of staying open late on the movie nights. People felt encouraged and safe. Other storefronts remained open on these nights. The area began to feel freedom and life again. One of the most responsible artists for the success was Stewart Stewart. He appropriately said, "there are two shifts in South Beach. There's nine to five. And then there's nine to five."(Wisser 1995.)

Paninoteca, **809 Lincoln Road** is always favored by locals. When you ask a local where they eat on Lincoln Road, the answer is almost always Paninoteca.

Before you hit the towering Mediterranean style office building with the ceramic tile roof, you'll unknowingly pass another landmark. The low-lying Mediterranean-style clothing store used to be more than fashion. In 1929 it originally housed one of the most prominent and fashionable stores of quality for women, **Bonwit Teller**. They later relocated across the pedestrian mall next to the current Victoria's Secret. Bonwit Teller was famous for providing high end, quality women's clothing, as well as paying their buyers and executives above-average salaries.

At the turn of the century women's clothing wasn't readily available like today. Bonwit Teller changed that for thousands of women looking for quality. Paul Bonwit, started in a different manner than most stores. He didn't birth the concept; it came from a lady by the name of Blanche Hagedorn.

In the early 1900s Blanche saw a problem in the four week wait to have a dress made. Many ladies were kept away from grand galas because their dress wasn't completed in time. Blanche put together a valise filled with dresses, visited the local women and sold them a dress. She then tailored the dress on the spot. Paul Bonwit saw potential and bought the idea from Blanche.

Blanche passed her good business sense onto her son, Horace Hagedorn who is the founder of Miracle Gro.™

Patterned floors show design incorporates all elements and areas.

The parent store for Bonwit Teller was located on 5th Avenue in New York City where it lived for many years, Lincoln Road was subsequently named the 5th Avenue of the South. The NYC location was bought by Donald Trump, demolished, and turned into the original Trump Tower.

After the quality women's clothier relocated it was occupied by Sak's Fifth Avenue, who also later moved across the street by the Euclid grass oval. After Sak's, the spot was home to Sarah Weinstock. In 1929, this was *the* place to shop on the Lincoln Road Mall.

The Saks Department Store made quite a stir with the ever going battle that has ensued in Miami Beach. The graceful transformation of progress that is generally accompanied by bulldozers and demolition has repetitively met the battle with The Preservation League. The fight has been emotional, expensive, time consuming, and at times a loosing battle. The efforts of **The Preservation League** have done indescribable wonders for the area.

After Saks lived on the road for twenty-five years, the profits grew slim. The area became depressed, shoppers dwindled, and the shop decided to close their doors and relocate further up the beach. With the saving attitude The Miami Dade Preservation League lives by, they acted on preservation. They stressed the beach was only going through a tough time and was making a comeback. Patience was necessary as the slump passed. In November 1979 the Miami Dade Preservation League went well beyond kindness and threw a splendid party encouraging the store to stay. The Ball On The Mall included an orchestra and a swing band but the effort was unsuccessful. Saks did not sign a new lease, instead they moved further north up the beach. The League did their best but in the end it was the financially responsible decision for Saks. It was only a short time later during the following year that the excessive crime hit. If Saks had stayed they would have experienced a bad area turn shameful when a few months later the boatlift arrived.

The reality was profound. The time of The Fairy Godfather, E.H.R. Green, was gone. Green was an eccentric who often waved his twinkle wand on stores with his presence. Mr. Green was the heir to well known financial tycoon Hetty Green who was commonly known to never waste a penny, well alone a dime. She made her fortune on Wall Street and bundled it with her family's whaling fortune and left it to her son. He was not such a tightwad.

Green had one leg, was shaped much like a fireplug, and caused a shopping spectacle two to three times each season in the mid-1930s. He traveled with his Boston terrier, decked in jewels and elaborate sweaters – yes, sweaters on a dog, in Florida. The Boston terrier is a derivative of the Bulldog, known for his fierce aggressive strong nature, muscular build and testosterone aura. Hmm... jewels, and sweaters...The Fairy Godfather loved to shop and had his limousine pull right up to the front door of his chosen store. Green never left the limo with its specially made extra large doors, glass roof, refrigerator, and full bed inside. (Redford 1970.)

The chauffeur parked the pleasure cruiser in front of the store and requested the staff. They came to the back window of the elaborate princess car and presented swatches and dress designs. Green would consistently purchase $500.00 worth of little girl dresses. The receiving party of the mystery dresses was a solid mystery that created quite a stir. (Redford 1970.)

Sewell's was one of the finest men's haberdasheries in town.

At **845 Lincoln Road** you'll find the location that formerly housed **Sewell's**. John Sewell was one of the most influential pioneers of Miami. He came to Miami in 1895 through Henry Flagler's railroad. He worked for Flagler as a regular day laborer where he was employed with the laying of the railroad tracks. He soon was put in charge of several men. While working the railroad he opened up a mercantile store, a commissary as he put it, in one of the train cars. In this car he supplied the men and any needs of the area. He saw good success with the mercantile but wisely kept his day job.

Sewell worked for Flagler up in the West Palm Beach area and described his position with confidence. "My personal camp consisted of four box cars, one for myself and commissary boss, one for the cook and dining car, one for the train crew, and one for the commissary car. Here is where I earned my first thousand dollars, making it out of my commissary." (Sewell 1933, 4.)

Near West Palm, he and his men leveled high sand dunes and filled in mushy areas prepping the ground for the railroad line. When Henry Flagler decided to move the line to Miami (then known as Fort Dallas) he asked John Sewell to lead the group, fire the unneeded men, and gather up the required necessities for the project in Fort Dallas. Their objective was to extend the line to Fort Dallas and build a hotel, The Royal Palm Hotel. At that time only a select number of small dwellings existed here. The established homes were sizable mansions owned by Julia Tuttle, F.S. Morse and the Brickell family.

After meeting with Flagler on the plan to lay track to Miami, Sewell pulled together 12 of his men out of the 209 from the West Palm job. John Sewell had his brother E.G. with him as the two men ran the mercantile store together. The plan was E.G. would run the store while John was putting up the hotel and railroad.

During that time, the land was overgrown with brush, rampant with vermin, and sparse on luxury. The local drugstore was over 100 miles away. It was naked undeveloped countryside.

On site these pioneers ate bread, bacon and grits. That's what they had – every meal. Breakfast... Lunch... Dinner. Bacon. Bacon and bread. Grits and bread. Grits and bacon and grits and bread and bacon. There was nothing else. It was a choice of grits, bacon or bread. The meager options sort of took the joy out of hearing the dinner bell. That was until one day when a fabulous treat rolled into their camp.

Somehow someone got their hands on eggs and a can of meat. The men feasted like kings, some even had two omelets. It was a true celebration – until they figured out the canned meat was tainted with botulism.

The hotel the brothers stayed in was high-class compared to the worker's tents but it wasn't the Ritz Carleton by any description. Wood wasn't readily available, making the rooms sort of... open to the elements in places. The hotel was so young there were no stairs to their shared second story room. They came to build a railroad and hotel, so they stepped up and built a ladder for their room. (Sewell 1933, 25.) It wasn't so bad, until the food poisoning set in. Up the ladder, down the ladder, puke, puke, puke. Up the ladder, down the ladder ...

John Sewell didn't get sick but his brother took a heavy dose. John, in his earlier days, spent time studying medicine so he did the best he knew. He grabbed his brother, limp and lifeless, and poured salt down his throat. He repeated the effort every five minutes until a bit of color filled his brother's cheeks. Then he hauled his brother over his shoulder and carried him up the ladder. They all woke up the next morning and went to work. (Sewell 1933, 36.) From there on bread, bacon, and grits looked inviting.

After the hotel and railroad were completed the two brothers remained in Miami and refocused their attention on the mercantile business as well as developing the town of Miami. According to John Sewell, The Hurricane of 1926 ruined him financially. He pulled himself up by the bootstraps, went back to work and continued on with business. He admired Carl Fisher saying, "I consider Mr. Fisher second to Mr. Flagler as Florida's greatest benefactor." (Sewell 1933, 197.)

Different building styles are pulled together through paint and soffits.

John Sewell was active in the presidential race for Franklin D. Roosevelt and present for the assassination attempt on FDR. Sewell saw the political process a little differently form that day forward. After the incident, the story unfolded to include the Miami Beach Dog Track. The assassin lost $200 in his bets, causing him to act on his lifelong dream to kill presidents and kings.

Al Capone, the famous mobster loved by the people because he brought gambling and booze to town during Prohibition held major controlling interest in the Miami Beach Dog Track. It was thought that Al Capone was behind the assassination attempt.

The Dog Track, located at South Point Park, right on the Government Cut inlet, was successful as gambling laws were adjusted in 1929. Restrictions became more gambling friendly.

Intermixed with the elderly people slowly walking the streets with their walkers and canes came big burly men establishing gambling rings while packing guns. The gangsters toked on heavy cigars and slung aggressive tongues loaded with abrasive language and little fear of the law, while the elderly sat on their porches in their lawn chairs and watched. The vast numbers of concrete porches filled with elderly in chairs gave the whole beach the nickname of God's Waiting Room. It's a painful dichotomy that God's Waiting Room was filled with drug smuggling, alcohol concealing, and bookies.

Recently, Capone's property was sold in 2006, according to Fiesta Tours, to Bill Gates for $20 million dollars. Gab around town says Jennifer Lopez's residence is the former site of Capone's house however her aerial plat doesn't match the plat Capone owned. Gate's does. This places the computer genius just doors away from Shaquille O'Neil's bed and around the bend of the island from the famous doctor with the largest estate in the area. Inventing Viagra served him well. Ahhh... the making of Miami.

A consistent source of gruff was directed on Al Capone and originated from the Sewell brothers. When the founding pioneers were establishing the area for business and trade, the goal was more to please the customer – the ever-valuable tourist – than to set up any religious moral ground. Rum Runners and bootleggers came over mostly from Bimini and the Bahamas to unload their much-desired sauce. It was so common at the time that if you weren't a bootlegger yourself, you were well acquainted with one and knew where to find him. In the battle to keep up with the lawbreakers, the Coast Guard fleet was increased from one ship to thirty-one to enforce Prohibition. Liquor raids, confiscations, and finding the local still was just another day.

The Sewell store run by the brothers was a symbol for moral high ground against the fight between Capone and his henchmen, the Dog Track, Prohibition and gambling. The brothers were politically active and prominent men of the community. They stood for something and everyone knew it. They actively fought to have Al Capone and his mobsters relocated.

Sewell's, the store that existed here on Lincoln Road was part of the chain started by the brothers. This store grew from the original Miami location that sold only shoes, this storefront carried much more. The look of the building when Sewell's was here was exactly the same as it is today. Both brothers were leaders and served as mayor for the city of Miami.

Sewell's was very much a family business, run and operated by multiple generations. One day when Uncle Ev Sewell was gone and nephew Jack Sewell was in charge of the store, a very well tailored man arrived. It was common to have such a man of high quality attire and stature shopping in the store. After all, it was a well-known men's haberdashery with garments of superior quality.

The very well tailored man made a substantial purchase. Nephew Jack wanted to encourage repeat business so he added a complementary belt and hat to the gentleman's bag as appreciation for his purchases. It wasn't until later that Jack Sewell found out the well-tailored man was Al Capone. Capone was so touched by the affectionate gesture that he and all his business associates shopped endlessly at Sewell's. (Kleinberg 1985.) Jack did his absolute best to keep the information from his uncle. At the time Ev Sewell was a prominent member of Miami's Chamber of Commerce.

Across the street from Sewell's was another very prominent building. It, however was not known for selling clothing to Al Capone on the hush, hush.

The Van Dyke Café, located at **846 Lincoln Road** is a restaurant downstairs where it spills out into the sidewalk. More than a few locals have said the food's not that great unless you stick to the hamburgers and the chocolate soufflé. Fair warning it takes forty-five minutes to prepare the chocolate dessert, which makes it the perfect people watching dessert. The locals that said they eat there are also the locals that used to work there, a sure sign of a clean kitchen.

Upstairs, is a more festive joint rocking away with the swaying, toe tapping tunes of jazz. The bathrooms are located upstairs so you'll catch some rhythm whether you pay the jazz cover charge or not but beware and be prepared, there is a cover charge. After all, this is Lincoln Road where only one thing is free. See if you can find it.

Jazz plays a very big part of South Beach and Lincoln Road. It represents freedom of the times. Jazz is Deco. Art Deco was born during the growth of the jazz movement, the machine age and the jazz age formed a bonding union. The style and movement was all about going somewhere.

The building itself is one of the oldest on the road. The history dates back to when the island was first being settled and was undergoing the transformation of swampland into a booming metropolis. This end of the island was notoriously swampier than the eastern end. Seeing a dredge, or two, on the bay scooping up sand to fill in the land was a common site in this direction.

Pilings were positioned, break walls were made and sand was filled. One island is still stuck in this transforming formation frozen in time off the south side of the 41st Street Bridge. Progress was halted in the early stages and now the shaped and unfilled island stands as a gang handout for roosting pelicans.

The Fisher offices now stand as a preserved landmark.

The Van Dyke Café building was created as offices for the real-estate and business pioneer, Carl Fisher. The Fisher Offices building was built in 1924 and designed by August Geiger, the same man who designed the bank building that now houses the Banana Republic store. He was known for his Mediterranean Revival architecture. Mediterranean Revival was a more eclectic form of architecture that ran a span from 1917-1935. The style was a group marriage between designs from Europe, Spain, Italy and France. Mediterranean Revival, donated to the world primarily by the Italians, is commonly used in tropical areas for several reasons. Mediterranean Revival is made up of concrete materials, making the structure more moisture resistant. In contrast, wood works like a sponge in humid temperatures and doubles as a condominium for bees. The strength of Mediterranean Revival buildings as a whole is enormously strong giving it the ability to withstand hurricane force winds. If damage does occur, it is relatively easy to patch the laceration. The structure can withstand hard-hitting sun and rain, yet it remains cooler in the penetrating heat. Mediterranean Revival commonly uses landscape filled courtyards, patios, fountains, hand painted tiles and wrought iron. Most importantly, there's generally a cozy meeting place designed specifically to enjoy a meal or glass of wine.

This is one of the few styles of architecture that makes the effort to incorporate all five senses, indirectly making the structure more relaxing and comfortable. At the time the building was designed, air conditioning did not exist. All sides of the building are designed around cross ventilation encouraging every ounce of a cool breeze. In a vacant state, standing as a naked shell, you can see clear through to the other side of the structure.

The building, named The Lincoln Building, is today commonly referenced simply as The Van Dyke Café. At the time the building was built, the land was open and undeveloped. Few houses and structures existed giving the view of palm trees, sporadic grass and sand as far as the eye could see. Carl Fisher was in the mad, yet sophisticated and controlled dash to sell his properties, which stretched to the North, West and East.

The view from Fisher's office encompassed the bay to the ocean.

Awnings were added in recent years.

Carl Fisher had the building equipped with an elevator to the top floor where his office was located. The balcony worked more like a look out tower for perspective buyers. After seeing the property on the ground a salesmen would bring the potential buyer up to the balcony. This would enable a sky view of the area and property, including the bay and ocean. After seeing such a beautiful breathtaking sight the potential buyer was taken back inside the office to sign papers on the purchase. This is how Carl Fisher sold over 3,000 properties. At the time, the Dow Jones Average was 134.

After the Fisher Offices were built, the city passed a new ordinance stating height restrictions to six stories. This was clearly not held firm in the way of variances and legal adjustments in later years. It is also the reason why the majority of buildings in the middle of the island are only a few stories tall.

The original elevator is still working today as the oldest working elevator on Miami Beach. In true South Beach form, the top floor is occupied by a **modeling agency**. Head model booker Monica Valiati said, "Models are often rescued by firemen on a consistent basis when the elevator gets stuck." This is a traditional day's work in South Beach for the firemen – rescuing trapped models, impatiently waiting to be released from the hot lift.

While Carl Fisher was stationed here, he eventually encountered financial difficulties. Combinations of factors were to blame. As always he was spread thin with his numerous projects. He diversified with investments in many properties, buildings and cities. According to his wife, Jane, he had roughly twenty-seven personal houses. He was also juggling miles of land, over 400 acres on Miami Beach and the 9,000 acres in New York at Montauk where he was planning the summer playground to complement Miami's winter playground theme. His estimated worth of $100 million was swallowed up by the difficult time. The Stock Market Crash of 1929 affected his holdings as well as directly caused the banks to fail, taking his money with them. When you add in The Great Depression when land sales turned stagnant, his dream ended.

For a time Carl Fisher still came to his office, even though financial difficulties were beyond control. He was an achiever with unstoppable brain-power. Inventions were bubbling in his head like a pot ready for spaghetti. He worked with his crazy early ideas of a room on wheels that could house people, dressing rooms, sitting areas, kitchens, and even bathrooms – all with the ability to travel the highways. He, along with a friend Charles Kettering, also toyed with the concept of a diesel engine, designing and reconfiguring different arrangements. At the same time, he put together plans for prefabricated houses- probably stemming from seeing the Sears and Roebuck houses on the island as the only ones to survive the hurricane of 1926. He configured a plan to save on costs by producing multiple pieces like wall or doorframes at one time. He then hoped to put them all together with his still surviving lots. On top of all that, he realized the power of the sign he used in NYC with the bathing beauties advertising the sun in the middle of winter. He orchestrated plans for the billboards lining the then growing highways. (Fisher Papers) In this office, during his financial decline, he wrote letters presenting his ideas to companies. Then he came to check the mail, day after day. He dictated more letters, sent more queries and continued to check the mail.

He hoped for some activity, anything to give life in his blood again.

While he waited, he drank.

The face on the façade could be mistaken for a Carl Fisher rendition.

Carl G. Fisher Properties held the name plaque the width of the building where the awnings now rest.

In the meantime he kept in contact with the few remaining friends who stuck by him even though his financial situation had drastically changed. One of those dear friends was his long time companion and confidant John LaGorce.

LaGorce was the Vice President of the National Geographic Society and editor of *The National Geographic Magazine*. He was the key correspondent to the magazine in the connection with Amelia Earhart and was thoroughly pulling for the young lass and her groundbreaking flight around the world by pulling the magazine's support for her flight. (LaGorce 1935, 1936.)

John LaGorce was a solid friend of Carl Fisher's from the very start of their interactions. He stood by Carl Fisher through these tough times and made Fisher feel useful with advise. Through Carl Fisher's tough financial situation, he kept his sense of humor. LaGorce expressed deep disappointment that his young son dropped out of college and got married, Carl reassured him it was not the end of the world; "I think the kid is all right. He shows he does not give a damn for your opinions or advice, which is another indication." (Foster 2000, 294.)

Carl Fishers final working days were spent here in his offices corresponding with letters and working on his inventions all the while looking out over the land he made. Fisher never did receive a response from his ideas. Fisher sat in his office high atop the developing area with little left. His wife had left him and his money was gone, he was left with just his own thoughts. His building that once bustled with dozens of salesmen, property managers, and publicists, was now a quiet office. Carl Fisher moved his residence up the beach to a small house and died from a stomach hemorrhage brought on by the heavy drinking. In 1939, Carl Fisher's pallbearers were Walter Chrysler, Bernard Gimbel, Frank Sieberling and William K. Vanderbilt. (Stofik 2005, 258.)

Walter Chrysler was famous for the Chrysler Corporation and the manufacturing of the Plymouth, Desoto, and Dodge. DaimlerChrysler cars would later make Mercedes Benz. Bernard Gimbel was famous for the development of the Saks and Company department stores. Frank Sieberling, Fisher's neighbor in the house across the street from the Shadows, was famous as the tire king acclaimed with several tire companies including, Sieberling Rubber Company, Goodyear Tire and Rubber, and Fulda Tire Company. William Vanderbilt was from the prominent railroad family and owner of Fisher Island.

Upon his death, Carl Fisher's long time friend, Will Rogers said of him, "Fisher was the first man to discover that there was sand under the water... (sand) that could hold up a real estate sign. He made the dredge the national emblem of Florida." (Fisher 1947.) Will Roger's also said, "Had there been no Carl Fisher, Florida would be known today as just the turpentine state... He rehearsed the mosquitoes till they wouldn't bite you until after you bought."(Fisher 1947.)

Carl Fisher considered himself a failure when he died.

The office building is one of the most beautiful structures on the island, not just Lincoln Road. If you take special notice around the side of the building you'll notice a bright red phone booth. What a hoot that phone booth. After countless inquiries making no headway on the history of the phone booth one elderly resident had the answer. As it turns out, phone booths were all over the place here on the beach, just like the rest of the country. They served their purpose but in terms of a grand triumph, they didn't come close. They weren't too successful for one main reason; they were hot.

In our sunshine they acted more like a self-cooker than a peaceful quiet place to make a call. It wasn't just a phone booth; it was more of a crock-pot. Elderly residents roamed the beach at the time of booth popularity. Seniors don't have the incredible need to make phone calls as they are out and about – especially when phone boxes for 911 were dispersed on countless poles. But at the time when cell phones didn't reside in every pocket and purse on the island, the phone booths were a needed asset. But this phone booth.... well, there's a funny thing about this phone booth – it's not one of those.

It's not even from here. As a matter of fact... it's not even American. Justo Varela says, "It's English style. The owners of the restaurant brought it over form England. They brought it over in the mid-'90s." In true Lincoln Road style, it's not just a phone booth; it's a great piece of art.

The English phone booth houses a working payphone.

Chapter 9
Cross Over Jefferson Avenue

On your walking tour it's important to remember to stay on top of the sidewalk as you walk. For, "in Florida, anyone found underneath the sidewalk will be found guilty of disorderly conduct."(Lindsell-Roberts 1994.)

At this area, Carl Fisher made this another monumental location back in the early part of the century. He "erected a private school at the corner of Lincoln road (sic) and Jefferson ave (sic). This building was later moved."(Donated clipping Historical Museum.) This school was open long before any public school on Miami Beach. At that time the children who did not attend the private school rode their bicycles over the wooden bridge to Miami for school each day. The Eunice Martin School was where the first congregating church body met before the Community Church on Drexel and Lincoln Road.

In the '80s with the triggered crime spree, this area of Lincoln Road was especially hard hit. From here over to the bay people were seldom seen. According to many locals, it was the place to rollerblade because you could make it through with out running into any people. Add to that the obstacle course designed by the trees and protruding root systems that broke up the concrete and the rollerblade course became a challenge. As soon as night engulfed the road, it was best to be indoors. From here to the bay drug dealers did their best business.

At one point in time Bonwit Teller moved from across the street, by the current Van Dyke Café, to this location at **901 Lincoln Road** where the current **Victoria's Secret** resides.

Victoria's Secret doesn't whisper on Lincoln Road.

This site was a famous location for another publicity photo, however it wasn't led by Carl Fisher. Well, it was, but not in a direct way. Pictures from this spot showed marching military men in their squadrons covering the whole length of Lincoln Road, from the ocean to here. The solid wave of marching feet, rhythmic singing and awesome strength was such a popular sight that it became a post card of the time.

In 1942, eighty-five percent of the hotel space was used as **WWII barracks**. Half a million troops were stationed in Miami Beach. They trained at the beach and on the golf courses. Here is where they marched. Back when Lincoln Road was a road, not a pedestrian mall, the soldiers took up the whole street. A steady sea of marching military personnel stretched from here to the shore. The picture silently shouted, MIAMI BEACH SUPPORTS OUR UNITED STATES SOLDIERS OF SERVICE.

Carl Fisher, during the time of unrest of WWI, sent an invitation to the U.S. Government asking them to use the area for whatever was needed. This created the precedent for troops using Miami Beach hotels as bunkhouses. Miami Beach was the single prominent location in America with the largest collection of available housing at the time. Speculation has been made that the troops kept life in Miami Beach where otherwise the city would have suffocated during the bleak time of war. Tourism clogged to a trickle during World War II.

During WWI, the military took over Bayshore Golf Course, that opened in 1923, as a training facility. Carl Fisher charged a rental fee of $1.00 a year. Three golf courses became one for their purposes. The military men were commonly seen practicing grenade launches and exercising at the course. The troops took over 22 Miami Beach hotels. The Navy took over Columbus Hotel.

Further up the beach on Collins Avenue was another popular training ground for the World War II troops. The rifle range set up residence on the sand dunes in Bal Harbour. Troops fired their practice rounds straight into the ocean.

"Truck convoys rolled through Miami Beach 24 hours a day. There was no let up as would-be pilots were put through six month courses in six-weeks. (The city was known as) the major army pilot training center." (Bramson 2005.)

The area was not only used for training, it was also a common stop over between assignments for personnel. The army of men fighting for freedom in World War II saw paradise on our grounds while they were here. Many soldiers enjoyed the area so much that they moved their families here after the war.

"Nearly 500,000 men, including matinee-idol Clark Gable, took over 300 hotels and buildings for housing and training headquarters under the Army Air Forces Technical Training Command. By the time the war ended, one-fourth of all Army Air Force officers and one-fifth of the Air Corps' enlisted men had been trained in 'the most beautiful boot camp in America'."(Camp Miami Beach WW2.)

The city was proud to serve her country, as well as relieved when the war effort came to a close. Shortly thereafter, new life was breathed into these solid storefront walls. A new, welcome neighbor joined the mix when young, agile, graceful, and toned bodies frolicked.

In 1986 the **Miami City Ballet** with nineteen dancers, practiced here in the same storefront windows of the naughty nighties at **909 Lincoln**. "The corner store had expansive windows... Villela (sic.) (the dance teacher) decided to keep the windows uncovered. Pedestrians would stop and gaze at the dancers working at the bar, pirouetting, and leaping across the floor. Sometimes the observers danced along or applauded when a number was finished." (Werne 1987.) Edward Villella and wife, Linda, former Olympic ice skater and key contributor to the very first Special Olympics, now teach behind the library on 22nd Street. The 63,000 square foot building is filled with fifty-two company dancers, thirty unpaid professionals, and 375 students. Edward Villella has received countless accolades as the one single man who changed the world of dance for male dancers. He recently celebrated his seventieth birthday by dancing in Don Quixote.

At **910 Lincoln Road** was the Temple King Solomon, were the crystal chandeliers remained from 1929 when it was built.

The rectangular fountain pushes strolling shoppers down the mall.

933 Lincoln Road is home to **Books & Books**, the long time resident is much loved by locals as a quaint shop that aims to please. The array of titles is exemplary of the variety of lifestyles and nationalities on the beach.

These shops make up the **Sterling Building**, originally built in 1928 with Mediterranean style architecture. At that time the structure was two separate buildings. The building on the East side was the Packard showroom. The front was covered with large display windows for the cars. Alexander Lewis, architect of the building, had his office next to the Packard showroom.

The Sterling Building took its name by then owners Dick and Bookie Sterling. Their daughter, Mindy, was often the cute little belle-of-the-beach dressed in frills and posing with political figures was just another day for Mindy Sterling. As a small girl, she was voted, "Little Miss Heart Fund." (Bramson 2005, 95.)

After Mindy Sterling grew up, she moved out to California where she acted in a few sitcoms as well as a select number of movie roles. Her acting career led her to become 'Frau Farbissina' the scheming and wicked costar to Mike Myers in the Austin Powers movies. (Bramson 2005, 95.) Farbissina branches from the Yiddish word meaning sourpuss.

Geometric in design, these artwork structures have been labeled cuff links.

The Sterling Building.

Mickey Wolfson, a great preservationist of the area, later bought the Sterling Building and established the structure to a higher quality. He housed the building with "stores, offices, (and) a private woman's dining club where following an obscure British tradition, all the waiters were called Michael." (Stofik 2005, 134-135.)

In 1941 the Sterling Building was redone into the Art Deco motif that remains today. At that time, the two buildings were joined as one with a floating glass block connector with the blue glass tile underlay. The colors change throughout the day ever so slightly if you watch closely.

Bowling at 1691 Michigan Avenue proves Lincoln Road has everything.

Chapter 10
Cross Over Michigan Avenue

Before you continue down Lincoln Road you need to visit the best ice cream factory in all of South Beach. Turn left on Michigan and stop at **The Frieze, 1626 Michigan Avenue**. Ice cream at The Frieze is a scoop of heaven in a cup. This popular chilling store makes its own ice cream every day of the week, including sugar-free ice cream that tastes just like the real stuff. In one visit your taste buds are sold, this is Breyers best competition on the market.

In front of the **Colony Theatre at 1044 Lincoln Road,** in the middle of the mall area is **a fountain**. This beautiful and picturesque fountain was designed and made by a very famous local artist, Carlos Alves. Alves specializes in creating beauty out of trash. (www.carlosalvesinc.com)

This is not the first image this fountain has portrayed. In truth, this is not the first Carlos Alves image the fountain has portrayed. The fountain was done and redone. The first Alves

Lapidus didn't originally incorporate the shade providing overhangs. They were later additions.

fountain was a lower fountain standing roughly a foot high. The underlay was a much darker background with a collection of muted colors floating through the darkness in waves of flowing color. It was beautiful. The current fountain is fun, exciting and alive. When children see the fountain they light up with giggles and glee. When adults see the fountain they see their inner child. The first Alves fountain was beautiful and sophisticated. One fountain, two makeovers, two styles, two impressions.

Square skylights create geometrical ceilings.

Square skylights create shade patterns as well as double the depth of structures.

Trash to treasure proves delight.

But is that the end of the story? Never!

This fountain had a life before Carlos Alves transformed it into a piece of beauty and style. This fountain had a story that involved numerous school children. In the '80s, an attempt to revive the area from the rampant crime was made. A local fourth grade class performed a school project right on this fountain. The area was filled with crime, the sidewalks were all broken, the foliage was overgrown, and the evenings were filled with drug deals.

The children were asked by their teacher to come to school with an old plate. The kids all went to the fountain on a school trip, broke up the plates, and cemented them in place. Each kid had his or her own mark on the fountain. It was a project of little fingers filled with multiple colors and patterns but most of all it was filled with love, something Lincoln Road lacked at the time.

Families would gather here to view their child's artwork. Visiting relatives were brought to this spot to see the difference their family was making. Most importantly, the kids were proud of themselves. They realized they could make a difference.

The locals in the area all knew each other. So the fountain became a place to sit and read the paper, have a cup of coffee, and visit with the regular crowd. The spray from the center of the fountain was often caught by a passing breeze and created a cooling mist. Residents that grew up on the beach tell the story from a different angle. They used to come at night with laundry detergent. They would pour it in the fountain, add some dye and watch all the different colors bubble up resembling a fizzing soda. The lights glistened in the bubbles and the colors darkened and lightened as the fountain spread the dye. Locals sat around the gurgling fountain with coffee in hand like it was the local campfire.

It's hard to say what political move changed the beautiful fountain made by little hands. The transformation met with many protesters along the way. It's a shame another fountain wasn't chosen so there could be two beautiful fountains.

The existence of the fountains are a symbol of engineering progress, especially for the time of installation. "More than 100,000 gallons of re-circulating water is used in the nine pools and illuminated fountains."(*The Miami Herald* 1960.)

The Colony Theatre stands as a landmark at **1040 Lincoln Road**.

This was the fifth working movie theater on Lincoln Road at one time. When it was open, the theater was clearly smaller compared to the big screens on the road. It contained 465 seats versus the Lincoln Theatre's 713 and the Carib's 2,200 seats. It opened for business in 1934 by Paramount. On a regular night, residents would attend the Colony Theatre, on a special night, the Carib.

One senior resident, Molly Weeks said, "I saw the *Sound of Music* there. Twice! It was big."

Nightlife at the fountain is relaxing as it begs a moment of peaceful rest.

The Colony Theatre entry is classic terrazzo Deco.

During the war effort on the beach, according to The Historical Museum, The Colony Theatre and The Lincoln Theatre's were used for the GIs to receive their assignments and watch training films.

In 1980 Samuel Kepnis, of the National Container Corporation, bought the run down theater in desperate need of repair. This was during the time the Marielitos were flooding onto our shores igniting the crime frenzy. He donated the landmark to the city of Miami Beach who then transformed the theater into a historical gem. The stage was rebuilt with a sprung wood floor, dressing rooms were added, a new updated air conditioner unit was installed, and a new electrical system was added. The carpet was made as a replica to the carpet housed in Radio City Music Hall. The acoustic system was enhanced and the front of the building got a face-lift.

The theater is widely known as a homosexual venue and hangout. The marquee frequently reads listings of gay and lesbian performers and productions. The Colony is not only famous in the homosexual community; it's popular in the pornography community.

The theater is a main course of the storyline and clearly shown in a "skin flick 'Blaze Starr Goes Nudist'. Blaze, weary from working under hot studio lights, goes to a movie to relax. She watches a film about a nudist camp in Homestead and immediately decides to become a nudist." (Atlmike 2005) Why filmmakers would choose Homestead which is known for farming and takes at least 45 minutes by car, instead of Haulover is a mystery. The Haulover Beach, which is known as a nude beach... err... naturist beach – where gawkers are discouraged – is only a quick skip up the street at 10800 Collins Avenue. If only the solid, God fearing, upstanding Quaker, John Collins knew...

On the south side of the street, stretching from Meridian Avenue to Lenox and Lincoln Road to 15th, was the home to Carl Fisher's **polo field,** the first polo field in Florida. (Lavender 2002, 122) Although short-lived, these polo fields, as well as the polo fields by The Flamingo Hotel were well used. Polo, at the time, was the up and coming sport of the wealthy. He spent, "$40,000 to bring clay from the Everglades, level it out, and plant the right variety of grass." (Foster 2000, 179)

The Colony Theatre.

When he was in the very early stages of putting together the field, the war took full affect. In Carl's true American helpful spirit he worked together with the government and offered the grounds for use as an airstrip. Hangers were built on the property and many planes spent their days and nights taking off and landing on these grounds.

"In April 1918, the Signal Corps leased it for $1.00 a year and built a hangar there. According to *The Herald*, it was the first polo ever played in Florida." (Redford 1970.) After the war was over the area resumed level play for polo. The clubhouse was located between Jefferson and Michigan again on this south side of Lincoln Road. The bleachers were set up for spectators running a vast length of the field with the overwhelming Flamingo Hotel standing in the background. The top dome of the Flamingo held the boldly waving American Flag, towering over the field as a backdrop of sorts.

Carl Fisher made a big production when the polo ponies arrived, naturally it was another free form of advertising. The horses were paraded in bold fashion across the wooden

Collins Bridge to the polo fields. Roughly 100 of the most fit, prime horses of superior athletic strength made up the force of the Miami Beach Polo Club. (Lavender 2002, 122.)

The ponies practiced every night at the polo grounds. Some visitors enjoyed watching them practice while many locals became accustomed to the crack of the mallet. The first game was played shortly after the grounds were prepared; Miami Beach Polo Club competed against Palm Beach.

Carl Fisher loved sports and he loved speed. He took to polo with passion and excitement. At the time, he was forty-six, making him farther along in years than other typical beginning polo players. He didn't care; he was having fun. In addition to his age, he was a bit heavier than most other players. With these two aspects, Fisher gave spectators the incredible feeling of, "I could do better than that guy." But all in all, he held his own, had a grand time, and was the most entertaining player as he fell off his pony in the middle of a game.

A friend of Fisher's showed concern and wrote him a letter. "You are no longer enrolled in the kindergarten class. Old Father Time has been walking along side you... You don't belong on a polo pony."(Fisher Papers) Carl kept playing. At the end of the season, they celebrated with a festival field day of races, games and even hurdles. They added games with more skill like "musical chairs on horses" where they set the chairs up in an oval. The riders walked around the chairs while mounted on their horses. When the music stopped, the riders had to dismount and lead the horse to their chair by the bridle and sit. In another contest, the rider raced to a marker, dismounted, lit a cigar, put on a costume including a parasol, climbed back atop the polo pony and raced back to the starting point. (Lavender 2002, 125)

When the second season came, not only did Fisher play but he organized one of the most monumental matches of all time. The Miami Beach Polo Club took on the Cubans. Before Castro's communist government, Carl Fisher extended a handshake ninety miles across the Atlantic to the south, inviting the Cubans to a match with the Americans. The idea was received with enthusiasm.

The Cuban team was made up of High Commanders and Commandants of the Cuban Army, plus an aid to the Cuban President. They were highly decorated men. It was a festive time of gentlemanly sport where even Rosie the Elephant was used to tamp down divots. (Lavender 2002, 125-127)

After the Cubans fairly won, they played into overtime just for sport. At that time one of the Americans – embarrassingly, the team leader – fixed the time clock. This was not in good fun but instead was to give the American team a chance to get ahead. Fisher found out and made an immediate decision to fire the player abruptly and harshly making a scene. This was Fisher's normal character; he was fair and detested those who weren't. He was the master businessman, professionally putting out fires as to not start a blazing inferno.

After the match, the Cubans and Americans partied with fortitude well into the night at Carl Fisher's swimming pavilion. They ate, danced, drank, smoked cigars and took tourist rides on Fisher's airplanes. The following night they had a large gala at Fisher's home. The match between the teams was so successful that the Cubans set up their own polo grounds in Havana.

Polo on these grounds proved later to be a point of heartache for Fisher. One of Carl's best friends was Julius Fleischmann, of the Fleishmann Margarine Company well known for their hearty yeasts and spreads. Fleishmann was an avid polo player who was skilled and known by his talent. One day, his luck turned when after a vigorous match he dismounted his horse and promptly died of a heart attack right on the field.

Polo is now free and open to the public on the beach in front of the Setai in April.

Chapter 11
Cross Over Lenox Avenue

Choose a shirt off the marble table built for deposit slips, try it on in the vault, and pay for it at the teller's counter.

At **1100 Lincoln Road** the **Banana Republic** store location was the former branch of the **Chase Federal Savings and Loan** and is historically protected. The solid structure was built in 1947 and designed by August Geiger, the same man that designed a great portion of Coconut Grove as well as the Fisher Offices where the Van Dyke Café now resides. Geiger favored a strong Mediterranean style of design overall. As one of the last buildings he designed he took a different angle on this building and put it together with Depression Moderne flair. This is an "architectural style which began when the Federal government's Public Works Administration commissioned the construction of new government buildings during the Great Depression. The government nature of most of the buildings required a more conservative approach and classical elements were reintroduced." (Root 1987.)

When **Banana Republic** bought the building, they were not allowed to change it because of the historical protection status. In creative fashion, they worked around their restrictions. You can now choose a shirt off the marble table built for deposit slips, try it on in the vault, and pay for it at the teller's counter. The store famous for the perfect white shirt and khaki shorts, now owned by the Gap, is now also famous for banking a shopping experience.

By the front door you'll notice a long grill that extends up the wall. This used to house the enormous air conditioning system used at the time. Underneath is a cubby with the original phone booth and water fountain positioned behind the original door.

The Banana Republic takes pride in telling their "Miami Vice" heritage. Outside their doors in the street of Lincoln Road a season one, "Miami Vice" episode was filmed. The filming of this episode was done before the city added the tree island of Royal Palms swimming the concrete wave. "Miami Vice," the art movement and numerous photo shoots by fashion magazines are all collectively credited with changing South Beach, specifically Lincoln Road.

"Miami Vice" came to the area in 1984 when crime was high and drugs were rampant. This area specifically was not lit well and proved dangerous. It was often filled with unsightly activity to the point where even the homeless people stayed away. This was the rough area of town. Vagrant types and tough guys with knives puffed out their chests and claimed this location as their stomping ground. As crime grew out of control in the 1980s, a nine pm curfew was established in attempts to create order. The only time a curfew is seen on the beach now is directly after a severe hurricane passes through, specifically for the purpose of looters.

When "**Miami Vice**" showed interest in using the beach for their show this was a feasible location for them economically. There was plenty of room to park their large trailers, rents were low- just a couple hundred dollars for a large two bedroom - and there weren't many spectators to cause a problem. Let's not forget the weather cooperated, it made financial sense. The city of Miami didn't agree. "The chamber of commerce, tourism officials, and civic leaders wrung their collective hands in dismay at the area's crime problems being glamorized on national television."(Stofik 2005.) The city officials were mortified thinking it would only show bad press. They feared the tiny trickle of tourists would dry up with the fear of getting shot. In result, more tourists came to see the filming.

The show helped the pull of spectators as well as beautified buildings. "Miami Vice" often painted various buildings in the vibrant pastel colors for the sake of filming. Tourism increased 10% as a direct result of filming with a continual climb shortly thereafter. Today drugs and crime in the city are different. City officials and police have been doing an incredible job of cleaning out the riffraff. "Over the past 18 years, 6,100 crack houses have been demolished. (Placing Miami as) no longer the nation's primary drug entry point. Miami-Dade has the lowest drug use of any major American urban centers. Drug use has been reduced by 50 percent since 1995 and is the lowest of any Florida county."(*Miami Monthly* 2006.) Those are hefty statistics in a short number of years. Hats off to our police force. The concept is poetic; a television show about drugs and crime can help solve the drug and crime problem.

A bit further is **Doraku**, a sushi restaurant famous with locals for the free sushi bar during happy hour.

As you finish up the stroll down Lincoln Road it's important to know the domination of the fashion impact located here. Lincoln Road has been fabulously known as experimental ground. This area has been commonly known as a shopper's showcase where designers test clothing and premier their new line. A trip to Lincoln Road has long been associated with a peek in the window of next season's fashions.

Before the road became a pedestrian mall, fashion show parades were held to present the styles of the coming year. Wartime bomb carrier chassis, thirty feet in length and eleven feet wide, were mobile stages. Models filled twenty dressed up carriers pulled by decorated tractors and lit by 3,000-watt generators. (*The Christian Science Monitor* 1948.)

In addition, the Fashion Guild on Lincoln Road creates a level playing field protecting consumers. One time a shop owner put a sign in his window displaying "Below Wholesale" prices preparing to unload some of his stock in a fraudulent fashion. The very next morning before any stores were open on the street, six other merchants were on the man's doorstep shutting down his twisted tactics of false advertising and misleading promotions. (Herndon 1954.)

One time a customer was bragging about a fabulous deal on his designer slacks. The neighboring storeowner knew the price of the material and knew the claimed price wouldn't cover the cloth not to mention the tailoring. He took the pants and sent them to the manufacturer for proof of the counterfeit material then forced the neighboring store to refund the customer (Herndon 1954).

On top of having the latest line of fashion available to you on Lincoln Road, you can find items available in few places around the world. One shop has been known to carry handbags of critical acclaim. Their colorful design guarantees you an original handmade item. When you're bored it can even generate a moment of contemplation. The bags are made from candy wrappers, potato chip bags and cookie packages. The brightly colored wrappers are twisted into weaving patterns that create a festive effect. Indians from Mexico twist the labels forming handbags, clutches and even belts.

Royal Palms show hourglass shaped trunk sections reflecting hurricane stressed years when the palm fronds were ripped off by heavy winds.

As you travel to the middle of the block you'll notice one of the original **street lights** that lit Lincoln Road in the center median. At a cost of $40,000 in the 1960s these were quality lights. (Herndon 1954.) "Fifty mercury vapor floodlight units aimed from the tops of 11 poles, 60 feet in height, all fitted with honeycomb-type grills to prevent glare. Wattages from 100 to 1,000 are located elsewhere in the structure. Bright enough to read a newspaper as if it were daylight." (*The Miami Herald* 1960.)

Direct and indirect lighting was designed through 71 under water lights and 311 additional lights run by starlight. At the time it was a major undertaking, the first project of its kind. The astronomic controls were ground breaking technology as well as the 25 miles of underground wiring. In addition they added electrical mainframes in four separate areas positioned strategically every other block. This was designed to prevent a black out engulfing the mall from circuit failure.

At the new **Regal Cinema's** located at **1120 Lincoln Road**, you'll find the latest idea flying through America. Church is now held at the local cinema instead of a church building. **The Lighthouse Church** runs their services at the cinema every Sunday morning. Pastor Wendell Fisher, a North Carolinian and New Yorker combined, leads the congregation with a come as you are concept. The worship is highly infectious as it is run by music director Sam Spears who performed on Shakira's Oral Fixation album. The church body is more of a family in itself, smaller on scale and more personal.

At the end of the block just before you reach Alton Road, you'll see an **empty parking lot** sandwiched between the Sun Trust Building and Alton. This space currently shows nothing but air, however a long ago it was an important part of the Lincoln Road team. This was the location of the **Miami Beach First National Bank,** founded in 1921. First National claimed they were first – first in name... first in size... first in service – as well as, the oldest and largest bank in Miami Beach.

The idea to promote the branch came in the form of a traditional Carl Fisher stunt. Someone decided to open a bank account in the name of Fisher's elephant, Rosie. Animals are often unpredictable no matter how well trained. Rosie proved this fact when on that day, she made history, yet again.

"Rosie was given a passbook and a five-dollar bill to hold at the end of her trunk and give to a waiting teller. In this strange marble barn where people flashed lights and cameras at her and put pieces of paper on her trunk, Rosie eased her anxieties with a long loud defecation that drove customers helter-skelter from the bank. It was, say all the old-timers, the biggest deposit that Miami Beach First National ever had." (Redford 1970.)

The concrete waves were added by the city a few years ago.

The Art Deco Regal Cinema has taken the place of the former 5 theaters on Lincoln Road.

Chapter 12
Alton Road

Standing on this spot at the end of the official Lincoln Road Mall you are experiencing a different setting than once existed. At the conception of the road, this location was peaceful, calm, and ... most of all ... quiet. The road was a white sandy coral. The Bermuda Grass was haphazardly grasping a foothold. Only one building existed in the immediate eyesight looking east, the bank on the corner. Further down was the seven story Fisher Offices, quite a way down the road. The wide road was lined with simple streetlights, no frills. The scene was simple. The **stone underpass entrance** to Lincoln Road was the item that made the impression. The underpass, built in 1921, consisted of miscellaneous rocks and limestone pieces fit together like a well-orchestrated dance arching over the four drivable lanes. The squared off top that stretched across the road was filled with triangular fittings purposely designed to grip creeping flowering vines as they reached across the underpass. Originally this was the official starting point to Lincoln Road with intentions of development from Biscayne Bay to the Atlantic Ocean. The top of the entrance underpass was shortly thereafter covered in vines draping down in elegant fashion. The sidewalk led through an open, arching personal stone entry with a mirror image of the entry on both sides of the road. Pine trees divided Lincoln Road from the rest of the area. The entry was inviting, simple and classy. It breathed elegance.

During the 1920s at least nine major movies were filmed here. Buchanan & Burton Real Estate advertised lots with 50-foot fronts on the ocean for $169.00. At that time the trolley system ran over the county causeway connecting the beach to the then bustling city of Miami. (Historical Museum pictorial display.)

As the road was transformed into a pedestrian mall, street crossings like this one, were lined with numerous two story poles topped with flags from surrounding countries. Lampposts did more than light the streets during this time. Posts displayed signs that represented different states of the union along with the state flower, state tree, and other facts including a defining year when the specified state joined the union. For example the sign for Idaho read: IDAHO, Statehood in 1890, state flower: syringa, The Gem state. When the "architectural firm of Lapidus, Kornblath, Harle and Liebman designed the mile-long parkway that cost $600,000," (*The Miami Herald* 1960.) state signs were left on the streetlights.

Trolley cars were inducted to transport the visiting guests and locals. "Two days after its launch, on Tuesday, December, 21 at 9:45 at night, the first trolley accident occurred on Miami Beach when a Garford bus going east on Lincoln Road hit the trolley car as it was going north on Alton Road. Damage was $200.00 to the trolley car, but no one was hurt." (Lavender 2002, 38-39.)

The trolley cars were put out of business a few years later by buses. Trolley cars are a separate issue than the **trams** that used to run on Lincoln. With the pedestrian mall transformation, trams ran the length of the mall shuttling shoppers from one destination to another. The trams were a mini version of a trolley; truthfully, they were powerful golf carts in disguise, each cart with soft benches running the length of a mini-flatbed. Some trams pulled a double bed enabling more riders. The prices fluctuated from a dime to a quarter and even ran for free for a time. Two challenges killed the tram; often times, people liked to walk, and political mudslinging accused alleged bribes. (Donated clippings Historical Museum 1962.)

One block south of Lincoln Road on Alton was a garage used as a holding tank for **Nazi prisoners-of-war**. Prisoners were put to work but reacted to the community like crass construction workers seeing women for the first time. The catcalls in German became a problem for the girls walking by on the sidewalks, especially those coming home from school.

One report described a young gal walking down the sidewalk behind two elderly women. A prisoner came forward, near the sidewalk, and began his normal loose-lipped surge of compost. Suddenly one of the elderly women turned on him and began to beat the prisoner, pummeling him with her handbag. She was snapping back at him in German, striking him with her tongue as well as her purse. Luckily for the prisoner-of-war, the American Military Policeman came to his aid. (*The Miami Daily News* 1945.)

Go Granny.

At the foot of Lincoln Road on the bay, Carl Fisher had a grandstand set up for boat regattas. Now the Regal Cinema remains the ending point of the mall area.

Must See Hits,
A Year At A Glance

January: Art Deco Weekend on Ocean Drive
February: Coconut Grove Art Festival – 3427 Main Hwy, over 300 artists, Miami International Boat Show
April: Polo World Cup 14-16 on the beach in front of Setai
May: Hip Hop Weekend – Memorial Day weekend, NOT FOR FAMILIES!
Miami Fashion Week, Latin America, May 6-10
June: Brazilian Film Festival, South Florida Boat Show
August: Miami Spice- selective restaurants offer their food at a set price-for 2006 it was $30.06 for a 3 course dinner, $20.06 for lunch, for some, that's well over half off regular price. Check the paper for participants, usually a full-page ad.
Usual Spice participants on Lincoln Road: Americana at the Ritz Carlton: 1 Lincoln Rd., Blue Door at Delano: 1685 Collins, Emeril's Miami Beach and Preston's at The Loews: 1601 Collins, Le Bon: 723 Lincoln Rd, SushiSamba: 600 Lincoln Rd, Yuca: 501 Lincoln Rd.
September: Miami Spice, High potential for waterspouts.
October: 14-16 Motorcycle Expo, Carnival Miami: parades, concerts, bands, fireworks; always great a sure fire hit - **Halloween Lincoln Road – *absolute entertainment! Never, never, never miss this event.*** Children trick-or-treat storefronts from 5-7, then the real fun begins when the children go home and the expert costumes appear.
December: Art Basal

Bibliography

Abbady, Tal. "Miami's zoo teems with new life 10 years after Hurricane Andrew," http://www.sun-sentinel.com/news/weather/hurricane/sfl_1992_ap_zoo_0.6698757.story.

Adams, Lisa. "Recycled purses wow NY, Miami." *The Miami Herald*, May 25, 2006.

Barwick, Margaret. *Tropical & Subtropical Trees and Encyclopedia.* Portland, Oregon: Timber Press, Inc., 2004.

Blonston, Gary. "19th-Century Cannon Found in Old Wreck." *The Miami Herald,* October 2, 1965.

Bramson, Seth. *Images of America Miami Beach*. South Carolina: Arcadia Publishing, 2005.

Browning, Michael. "Thieves Rob Mall Shops But Can't Steal Spirit." *The Miami Herald*, Tuesday, October 21, 1980.

Camp Miami Beach WW2, WWII Miami Beach Veterans, American Legion Post 346, http://www.miamibeachvets.com/

Cawthon, Bill. "2 Fast 2Fabulous." Promotex online articles, June 1, 2005.

"Change With Change—That's Lincoln Road System." *The Miami News*, Thursday, August 21, 1958.

Chase, Iris. *South Beach Deco, Step by Step.* Atglen, Pennsylvania: Schiffer Books, 2005.

The Christian Science Monitor. "Boston, Fashion Forecast for '49: Florida to Feature The Newest Look, Outdoor Style Show Set For Miami Beach Festival." Friday, December 10, 1948.

Donated Press Clipping, "Back in 1929, this was the main shopping area of Lincoln Road."

_____. "Beach Councilman Asks State Probe In Tram Franchise."

_____. "Hey, Let Go My Front Seat." Historical Museum of Southern Florida, Lincoln Road file, no source or date.

_____. "Merchants Happy? Well, Yes… and No."

_____. "Swamp To Swank."

_____. "Miami Beach Sees Another Dream Come True." *The Miami Herald*, Sunday, November 27, 1960.

Drefft, Bryan. Lincoln Theatre, Miami Beach, Florida, Cinema Treasures. http://www.cinematreasures.org/theater/3087,/4655/

Eiland, Darrell. "That's 2 Steps for Hall, 2 Great Feet for Mankind," Donated clipping, estimated *The Miami Herald*.

Fiesta Boat Tours.

Finkelstein, Al. "Dream Comes True, New Life, Dress For Lincoln Road." *The Miami Herald*, donated clipping.

Fisher, Jane. *Fabulous Hoosier*. New York: R.M. McBride, 1947.

Fisher Papers, from Carl Fisher to Mr. Roy D. Chopin of the Hudson Motor Car Company, April 30, 1928. Box 1.

Fisher Papers, letter to Carl Fisher from Bookwalter-Ball Printing Co., signature illegible, presumed to be Frank Ball, Box 10.

Fisher Papers, Historical Museum of Southern Florida.

Foster, Mark S. *Castles In The Sand, The Life and Times of Carl Graham Fisher*.

Gainesville, Florida: University Press of Florida, 2000.
George, Paul. *Florida, Yesterday and Today*. Morristown, New Jersey: Silver Burdette Company, 1987.
Geran, Monica. http://www.highbeam.com/
Herndon, Booton. "Lincoln Road: Boulevard In The Sun." *Esquire: The Golden Playboy*, February, donated clipping estimated 1954.
Hiaasen, Carl. *Paradise Screwed.* New York: G.P. Putnam's Sons, 2001.
HighBeamEncyclopedia.com/
http://www.aoml.noaa.gov/hrd/tcfaq/E12.html
http://www.avianweb.com/
http://www.carlosalvesinc.com/
http://dhr.dos.state.fl.us/services/sites/floridians/?section=m
http://www.geocities.com/keeksaccount/zangara.htm?200626.
Internet correspondence, Thomas W. Lamb II, 8-29-06, 9-8-06.
Kiser, Mel and Corky Irick. "Calling Miami Home." VHS, Southern Films, Inc., 1984.
Kleinberg, Howard. *Miami Beach, A History*. Miami, Florida: Centennial Press, 1994.
_____. *Miami, The Way We Were*. Miami, Florida: Vanderbilt Printing, Inc., 1985.
Krefft, Bryan. Cinema Treasures, Colony Theatre, http://www.cinematreasures.org/3085/
LaGorce, John. Purdue University Libraries, Archives & Special Collections, Letter 1935, Dec. 9, New York City to Dr. E. C. Elliott, Lafayette, Ind.; Letter 1936, Jan. 2, New York City to Dr. E. C. Elliott, Lafayette, Ind.; Letter from John LaGorce to Jack, no last name referenced @ 2 West 45th Street, New York City, Jan. 2, 1936.
Lapidus, Morris. "How Architect Explains Promenade." *Miami News*, August 21,1958.
Lapidus, Morris. *Too Much is Never Enough.* New York: Rizzoli, 1996.
Lavender, Abraham D. *Miami Beach in 1920, The Making of a Winter Resort, The Making of America Series*. South Carolina: Arcadia Publishing, 2002.
Lindsell-Roberts, Cheryl. *Loony Laws & Silly Statutes*. New York: Sterling Publishing Co., Inc., 1994.
McAuliffe, Emily. *Florida Facts and Symbols*. New York: Hilltop Books, a division of Grolier Publishing, 1998.
Miami Beach 411, Morris Lapidus Biography. http://www.miamibeach411.com/history/bio_lapidus.html.
Miami Beach Sun. "Lincoln Mall Construction Begins Aug. 1." Sunday, June 26, 1960.
Miami Daily News. August 1, 1962.
Miami Daily News. "New Beach Soldiers Developing Marksmen's Eyes." July 11, 1943.
Miami Monthly. "Miami Vice No More." August 2006, 6.
Miami Public Pages. "Franklin D. Roosevelt (Assassination Attempt)." Information released by the Federal Bureau of Investigation, U.S. Department of Justice under the Freedom of Information and Privacy Acts, http://digital.library.Miami.edu/gov/FDRAssn.html.
Nash, Eric P. and Randall C. Robinson Jr. *MiMo, Miami Modern Revealed.* San

Francisco: Chronicle Books, LLC., 2004.
"Nightlife and Recreation Clips form Miami Beach, 1940s-1960s." Courtesy of Louis Wolfson II, Florida Moving Image Archive.
Oral interview. Banana Republic store manager, May 21, 2006.
Oral interview. Dennis Leyva, Art in Public Places Coordinator for City of Miami Beach, August, 15, 2006.
Oral interview. George Neary, Associate Vice President of Cultural Tourism at Greater Miami Convention and Visitors Bureau, August 21, 2006.
Oral interview. Grace Calvani, November 14, 2006.
Oral interview. Herbert Tucker, May 21, 28, 2006.
Oral interview. Justo Varela, August 20, 2006.
Oral interview. Molly Weeks, August 23, 2006.
Oral interview. Pepe Menendez, July 26, 2006.
Oral interview. Rachel Speck, November 21, 2006.
Oral interview. Sam Spears, August 20, 2006.
Osgood, Charles. "Architect Morris Lapidus Died at age of 98." *CBS News Sunday Morning*, January 21, 2001.
Polansky and Aristides J. Millas. *Miami Dade Preservation League.* Miami, FL: Printed by Bayshore Graphics, Inc., 1994.
Potts, Jackie. "Lights... Camera... Pay Dirt." *The Miami Herald*, January 4, 1997.
Ringen, Honathan. "Lapidus of Luxury." *Metropolis Magazine*, http://www.metropolismag.com/html/content_0101/ml.htm.
Redford, Polly. *Billion-Dollar Sandbar, A Biography of Miami Beach*. New York: E.P. Dutton & Co., Inc., 1970.
Renault, Dale S. "NEW Planning Needed for Lincoln Road." *Miami Beach Daily Sun*, Sunday, April 14, 1963.
Root, Keith. *Miami Beach Art Deco Guide*. Miami Design Preservation League, 1987.
Sewell, John. *John Sewell's Memoirs and History of Miami Florida*. Miami, Florida: printed Lithographed and Engraved by The Franklin Press, Inc., 1933.
Silva, Helga. *The Children of Mariel, Cuban Refugee Children in South Florida Schools.* The Cuban American National Foundation, Inc., 1985.
Smiley, Nixon. "Concrete Road – or a Garden? Lincoln Road Mall Up to Voters Tuesday." *The Miami Herald*, donated clipping.
Stofik, M. Barron. *Saving South Beach*. Gainesville, FL: University Press of Florida, 2005.
Training Grounds Smoke Grenades, Course History, www.miamibeachgolfclub.com/
Voren, Howard. "Champions of Charm." http://www.proaviculture.com/conures.htm.
The Washington Post. "Famed Hotel Architect Morris Lapidus Dies; Known for Flamboyance." January 20, 2001.
Werne, Jo. "Deco Condo: Broadway Producer Expects a Hit With Revival of 1936 Building." *The Miami Herald*, May 31, 1987.
Wikipedia.
Wisser, Bill. *South Beach, America's Riviera, Miami Beach, Florida.* New York: Arcade Publishing, 1995.